Gretchen Hildebrandt

An Organic Inquiry Primer for the Novice Researcher

A Sacred Approach to Disciplined Knowing

Deah Curry PhD
Steven J Wells

Liminal Realities
Kirkland, WA

ISBN 978-0-7414-3078-6

For information:

Liminal Realities,
11410 NE 124th St
Kirkland, WA
Publishers@LiminalRealities.com
425-814-9083

Library of Congress Cataloging-in-Publication Data
Main entry under title:
An organic inquiry primer / Deah Curry & Steven J Wells

Includes bibliographical references
1. Psychology–Research–Methodology. 2. Transpersonal feminist psychology–Research–Methodology. 3. Sacred approach– Disciplined knowing. I. Curry, Deah. II. Wells, Steven J.

Published by:

INFINITY
PUBLISHING.COM

1094 New DeHaven Street, Suite 100
West Conshohocken, PA 19428-2713
Info@buybooksontheweb.com
www.buybooksontheweb.com
Toll-free (877) BUY BOOK
Local Phone (610) 941-9999
Fax (610) 941-9959

Printed in the United States of America
Published January 2013

Contents

Acknowledgments

I had never heard of Organic Inquiry until it was presented to me as a methodology option for a preliminary project to my doctoral pilot research by my committee member Jürgen Kremer, Dipl.-Psych., whose much appreciated expertise guided me gently through those challenging years and subsequent research.

I also wish to gratefully acknowledge my dissertation committee chair Ruth Richards, MD, PhD, and dissertation committee member David Lukoff, PhD, who took the risk of allowing me as a novice researcher to use an emerging methodology, and whose standards of excellence I tried to achieve.

I am particularly thankful to Jennifer Clements, one of the originators and authors of *Organic Inquiry: If Research Were Sacred*, (available at www.serpentina.com) for sending me an early unpublished manuscript outlining the role of the concept of traveling to the liminal, and a draft of her forthcoming book *Organic Inquiry: Research in Partnership with Spirit* so that I could have the latest information available from the source of this new approach to research in the human sciences. The work Jennifer and other Organic Inquiry co-founders Dorothy Ettling, Dianne Jenett, and Lisa Shields is truly pioneering in inspiring others to view research as a sacred endeavor.

Finally, I wish to give my deepest thanks to my research and writing partner Steve Wells for his pivotal role in being the integrity guardian for how we have used this methodology. This work has been well blessed.

~ Deah Curry, PhD
Summary, 2003

I am not an academic person, so when Deah first approached me two years ago to ask me to help her as a research assistant for her doctoral dissertation I couldn't imagine being able to adequately assist her. But, as she patiently explained what I would be required to do, I realized that I had the skills, if not the experience, to do as she asked. For these skills I humbly thank my many and diverse Spiritual teachers and mentors throughout my life. Using a methodology that intentionally invited Spirit in as a guiding principle was second nature to me.

Being a *practical visionary* has also been second nature to me. This project allowed me to bring my visionary aptitude to a practical wok by creating a template for research that will have tangible effects on those who use it and those who read the works written using it. Towards that end I wish to thank Mark Souder of Studio 403 in the Seattle area for his excellent work in the creation of the original edition of this book. He has given us a high standard to follow. I'm also very grateful to the folks at Infinity Publishing for their help in turning out such a high quality book. Their positive attitude and excellent support have been a big help to us.

Still, the person I thank the most for helping me accomplish these projects is my friend and associate, Deah Curry. Without her consistent support, encouragement and purposeful attention to my well-being I would never have been able to do this. Thank you Deah. I, too, have been blessed by this work.

~ Steven J Wells
Summer, 2003

PREFACE

We have been involved with the Organic Inquiry approach to qualitative research in the human sciences since Spring of 2000, having used the methodology in three separate but related research projects. As novice researchers ourselves, we realized early on that we needed more information than was available from the original sources on Organic Inquiry to guide us through the intricacies of complex research in human sciences.

Many times, in a need for concrete sequential formats, I (Deah) wanted a book that provided step by step guidelines for operationalizing the principles of an Organic Inquiry. Not that I would have followed such guidelines to the letter, but it would have been comforting to have some established points for my unique departures.

Many times during data gathering and analysis, we (Deah and Steve) wondered if what we were doing was going too far away from the intent and integrity of an Organic Inquiry, and wished we had more structure to guide us. And so, in that Spirit, this primer is born.

In developing a book for other novice researchers, our goal has been to lay out one possible way to apply the Organic Inquiry approach to disciplined knowing. We do not claim this is the only way to use the methodology. In fact, other ways have been successfully employed, as more than 40 doctoral dissertations and other research projects can attest to date.

Interested researchers are directed to the libraries of the Institute of Transpersonal Psychology and the California Institute of Integral Studies for help in locating Organic Inquiry dissertations.

My (Deah's) own dissertation is housed at Saybrook Graduate School and Research Center, and is also available for electronic purchase (with black and white photos) at http://wwwlib.umi.com/dxweb/gateway or on CD (with color photos) through our website http://www.LiminalRealities.com

We have also revised my dissertation as a trade book for the psychology and naturopathic medicine audiences. Titled *Healing Presence: Bodily Felt Experiencings of Transpersonal Connection in Naturopathic and Non-Clinical* Settings, this book is available from Infinity Publications website www.BuyBooksOnTheWeb.com, at Amazon.com, and through LiminalRealities.com.

This primer walks the student or beginning researcher through our perspective of the larger context of any Organic Inquiry as situated in its lineage and paradigm by its inherent belief system, and by its conceptualization of the relationship between humans and the sacred. In addition, issues that must be of concern to all serious researchers, such as concern for subjectivity, validity, and limitations, are explored in the context of an Organic Inquiry.

Several data analysis methods that might be useful in an Organic study are compared, and some specific questions about Organic Inquiry are addressed for the benefit of students and research supervisors alike. This is by no means an exhaustive set of data analysis methods that might be compatible with Organic Inquiry, but it is what we investigated before settling on content analysis.

Then, we describe how Organic Inquiry was applied in one major, complex, research study, and give the reader some suggestions for their own projects that allow much room for creativity and innovation while still sustaining the heart of what makes a particular project an Organic Inquiry.

Throughout the primer we offer tips and opinions designed to help the novice researcher feel more comfortable in rising to the challenges that Organic Inquiry presents. We have left space throughout the pages, as well as large areas at the end of each chapter for you to capture the ideas that will no doubt bubble up from the liminal domain as you read through this primer. Clearly, our advice comes from our own experiences, our own backgrounds and biases, and are not meant to suggest that ours is the only way to use this methodology. Novice researchers and faculty supervisors alike are encouraged to obtain a copy of the original source material for this methodology, as well as to tailor the methodology to their own needs. In this way, this innovative and valuable addition to human sciences research methodologies will remain rooted in its native ground, while also growing in unexpected—indeed, organic—ways.

Because this methodology calls different gifts and wisdom out of each of us who uses it, the more information that is shared among those of us following this approach, the broader become the possibilities for application of Organic Inquiry. We strongly encourage readers to contact us with questions that we might include on the Liminal Realities website or in future newsletter, as well as with your successes and dilemmas. In this way, you as the reader now, and as the soon-to-be Organic researcher, will be living and influencing the growth of Organic Inquiry as a methodology for the human sciences. Contact us at Publishers@LiminalRealities.com

CHAPTER 1

Introduction to Organic Inquiry

This book is written for the novice researcher who is considering using a Spiritually-based, innovative, and highly flexible qualitative methodology for a disciplined inquiry of a specific topic in the broad field of psychology, although students of other fields may also find it useful. We try to make no assumptions about the researcher's experience with or knowledge about research in general, or qualitative research in particular. Specifically, this book is a beginner's look at how and why one might propose and perform an Organic Inquiry.

Research is usually thought of as a process of "doing science." Stereotypically, we think of subjecting participants—whether animal or human—to some experimental conditions under double blind conditions, and counting how many times this or that occurs so that we can arrive at some statistically significant result that can be generalized to other populations with reasonable assurance.

In contrast, by seeking to know in-depth about the experience or experients of some concept or phenomenon as it is lived, the Organic Inquiry approach to human sciences research is exploratory and discovery oriented. In our opinion, it is especially well suited for investigating elusive topics, for questions that take the researcher into the unknown, and for concepts for which there is not yet an agreed vocabulary.

Because Organic Inquiry holds an assumption that all things are sacred and interconnected, it allows the researcher to find connections between things that might otherwise be thought separate. On the other hand, there is the potential risk that the researcher will start to see all the data as interconnected—a challenge that may create confusion, even though this may be true. This can lead one into tangential paths that may not be as centrally connected to the research as is first supposed. Thus, the methodology calls for a serious commitment on the part of the researcher to frequently examine the work one is doing to be sure it is both expanding the research to include all its possible limits, while at the same time staying within the stated boundaries of the research question.

Organic Inquiry as an Emerging Research Methodology

Organic Inquiry is a relatively new addition to the range of options for psychological research. Its genesis in 1994 is rooted in the desires of Jennifer Clements[1], Dorothy Ettling, Dianne Jenett, and Lisa Shields (1998)–who were all at one time associated with the Institute of Transpersonal Psychology in Palo Alto, California— to "find a sacred and personal voice... in research" (p. 114). As an emerging methodology, Organic Inquiry grows from its roots in transpersonal psychology, and from some specific features of feminist theory and Spirituality.

From transpersonal psychology, in which experiences of the sacred in everyday life as well as in exceptional events are commonly the subject of research, Organic Inquiry also seeks to use such experiencing of the sacred as a way of knowing. Thus in an Organic Inquiry, one incorporates engaging with the sacred in some manner during the operation of the research design through researcher preparations and attitude, in participant recruitment and selection, in data collection and data analysis, and in interpretation and final report.

---

[1] In accordance with the Organic Inquiry requisite for personal emancipation we use first and last names to indicate persons who have written about or performed Organic Inquiries. Others are referenced by the more standard practice of last name only.

Engagement could take the form of ritual, meditation, prayer, sacred dance, inspirational reading, or any of a number of personal Spiritual practices, primarily done by the researcher during preparation and analysis stages. Engagement by participants need not be extensive, and can be limited to—in effect—inviting oneself to have and contribute to an awareness of the sacred aspects of inquiry.

Jennifer Clements (2000, 2001), in revisions to the methodology, suggested a shamanic engagement that she called traveling to the liminal realm to gather information in the form of inspiration or guidance as well as research data. The liminal realm can be understood as the space between the mundane and the sacred, which in psychological terms could be viewed as the personal subconscious and collective unconscious domains. This feature of engaging with the sacred sets an Organic Inquiry apart from most other qualitative research methodologies although general engagement with subjective ways of knowing is a major feature of the Heuristic Method, (Moustakas, 1990), of Intuitive Inquiry (Anderson, 1998, 2000), and of Spiritual Inquiry (Rothberg, 1994).

From a feminist Spirituality, in which an honoring of the unfolding, embracing, intersubjective nature of the sacred has an aliveness to experients, Organic Inquiry shares philosophical ground with the worldview of indigenous societies, or what Tarnas, et. al. (2001) have discussed as the cosmic world, and what was termed deep ecology by Naess (1973), and as elucidated more recently by Maughan and Reason (2001). Aspects of feminist theory are also present in Organic Inquiry, such as operating from a *power with* or *power from within* (Starhawk, 1997) stance instead of the non-feminist model of *power over.* These features of feminist theory honor the sacred at work in everyday life, value participant's voices and the intersubjective nature of knowing as authentically expressed stories, and make explicit a goal of transformational (i.e., emancipatory) learning. [see Elias, 1997; Mezirow, 1997, 1998]

In our view, there are currently three models of the Organic methodology: the original five principles model, our modification of that to add a sixth principle, and a process model. The original five principle model includes the elements of the sacred, the personal, the relational, the chthonic, and the transformative. We added the element of the numinous to balance out the chthonic. The process model has as its emphasis traveling to the liminal, gathering data there, and returning to integrate it. These models are discussed in depth in a further section of this chapter.

Lineage of Organic Inquiry Among Other Methods

Clearly, Organic Inquiry intends to make us more conscious of the embodied nature of meaningful, lived experience. Explicitly or implicitly, it draws on kinship with the heuristic, narrative, and ethnobiographic approaches to knowing a topic in rich detail. Further, Organic Inquiry means to seek engaged dialogue and transformative learning rather than reductive results. The Organic Inquiry methodology is an exploratory and subjectively descriptive one, rather than a predictive, or even abstractly interpretive, method. In our view, it seeks to bring into the explicate order (Bohm, 1980) the meaningful stories of lived experiencing under investigation (Gendlin, 1997; Van Manen, 1990).

In considering this lineage, it also then becomes clear that an Organic study may benefit from borrowing various methods and procedures that have weathered the tests of time in some of these other approaches to human sciences research. Students and novice researchers in particular may find it comforting to incorporate, for example, the indwelling process of Heuristic Inquiry, the processes of ethno-autobiography (Kremer, 2003), or any of the narrative data analysis procedures in exploring what in-depth interview transcripts have to yield about an area of investigation, to suggest but a few options.

Epistemology, Cosmology and Assumptions

All research methods evolve. Organic Inquiry has already moved from its original five principles model of the sacred, the personal, the chthonic, the relational, and the transformative, to a three step process model of engaging the subconscious or the liminal realm, gathering information there, and returning to integrate it (Jennifer Clements, 2001). We would encourage novice

10

researchers to make use of both the principles and process models if what is desired is to achieve a rich descriptive study that never forgets that the researcher and researched are operating in a sacred manner, and in partnership with Spirit.

To understand the epistemology, and cosmology we believe are inherent to the Organic Inquiry approach to human sciences, the following section explains the five principles of the original model, and the one principle we have added in order to complete the cosmology, in our view.

Terms of Model and Methodology Defined

The original model on which Organic Inquiry is built consists of the characteristic principles of the sacred, the personal, the chthonic, the relational, and the transformative. We found that this model needs the addition of *the numinous* to give it balance, as explained further on. This reconceptualization further clarifies Organic Inquiry's position among research methodologies as strongly psychoSpiritual in its orientation. Definitions of the principles of the model have not been given in Jennifer Clements et. al. (1998, 1999; nor in Clements, 2000, 2001), except by descriptive example. Here, we first define each term as we use it, and then we give the original context from Jennifer Clements et. al., (1999).

The Sacred

We define the term *the sacred* as an attitude or atmosphere in which one is aware of, and respectful and reverential toward, the indwelling of Spirit—which we distinguish as the living energy of *the great mysterious.* This might be thought of as similar to a Taoist conception, as an ever-active catalyst that is life unfolding. In this sense, the sacred is a qualitative state of the presence of Spirit, while Spirit is an embodying creative force, or life-force energy.

Jennifer Clements et. al. (1999) described this principle of the Organic model as an aspect of expanded consciousness in which researcher or readers begin:

11

spading up one's old habits and expectations and achieving an ongoing attitude which respects and allows for the sacred to emerge....so that when the seed of the research is planted, it will find fertile conditions in which to grow....Doing this work requires honoring ourselves, our collaborators, our readers, and the context in which we work, as well as intentionally keeping ourselves open to the gifts of our own unconscious mind and those of the divine. (p. 14)

The principle of the sacred is positioned as the first aspect of the original Organic Inquiry model, establishing its outright difference from other qualitative methodologies. In doing so, Organic Inquiry claims its belonging to the participatory paradigm rather than the modernist view of the universe. To see research as sacred requires that we see ourselves and our interdependence as sacred as well.

In Jennifer Clements' (2000, 2001) revised model—with its shift to the three-part process construct of traveling to the liminal domain, gathering wisdom there, and returning to integrate it— Organic Inquiry's focus on the sacred is only slightly less emphasized. Further, the sacred is implicit in the revised model's stage of preparation in that the researcher "brings [her or his] understanding into partnership with Spirit so that liminal wisdom may come to light" (Jennifer Clements, 2001, p. 38). This partnering with Spirit, we contend, is both an embodiment of the sacred, and a creation of a consciousness of sacredness. We have found that it is necessary to not only bring this awareness to the research, but to actively engage this concept in one's daily life, as we move through the various processes of the study.

The Personal

The word *personal* can be defined with common parlance as that which belongs or has meaning to a specific person. In an Organic Inquiry, it is the researcher's personal story or passionate interest that serves as the seed for the study such that "her or his subjective experience of the topic becomes the core of the investigation....and a filter for the other stories she or he will gather" (Jennifer Clements et. al, 1999, p. 26). Also, an Organic Inquiry emphasizes the hope that the eventual readers of the final research report will engage with the stories and findings in the report in a way that serves to re-enliven their own experience. Because an Organic Inquiry is transpersonal in its basic philosophic orientation, here the principle of the personal is intended to relate to the individual person.

In this regard, an Organic Inquiry is parallel to the Heuristic Method (Moustakas, 1990) in using the researcher's own experience as the impetus for a research question, and as a guide throughout the research process. In our studies, we continually returned to our own stories to maintain our surety that we were engaging the methodology from this standpoint.

The Chthonic

The word *chthonic* means *in the earth,* and has come to connote something dark and mysterious, or to imply a shamanic type of underworld. Chthonic in the way Jennifer Clements, et. al. (1998, 1999) use the term, implies a domain of unformed potential that can also be understood as a realm of *becoming.* Clements and her methodology co-founders, and their followers, have used *chthonic* to refer to the contents of the subconscious, a time-place in which the roots of the research grow in unexpected directions and ways, not to be contained by the original (and presumably incomplete or imperfect) research plan.

If viewed, as we do, as akin to the shamanic underworld as simplified by Walsh (1990), the chthonic could also be understood as a "place of tests and challenges" (p. 147). In other shamanic models, such as the Mayan, the underworld can also be the home of certain guides and allies. It is here in the chthonic of the Organic Inquiry that researchers' instincts guide the growth of the project, where they battle to overcome doubts and worries, and learn to trust the guidance they receive, and to trust themselves as disciplined knowers.

It also serves to literally ground the research, and continually reminds one of the necessity of keeping the work rooted in the sacredness of the earth and the actual ground of being where we all live our daily lives. As such it is not only a metaphysical but also a physical realm.

13

Although the relationship of the chthonic to the sacred is not spelled out in the source material on Organic Inquiry, by positioning the chthonic as the third principle, the implication is that it is something separate from the sacred. This positioning is consistent with some Spiritual systems that do not conceive of the dark being part of the light, but rather a separate domain.

We would tend to take a more wholistic, perhaps even Taoist or shamanic, view that the chthonic is an indivisible part of the sacred that is of mystery, uncertainty, unknownness. It is the chaotic domain of creation, the potentiated germination of healing's roots in growth, beauty, connection, and community (Richards, 1990, 1996, 2000, 2001; Runco & Richards, 1997).

The intention of this principle in the original model was to convey that an "Organic Inquiry has an underground life of its own...the method is often called upon to evolve and change over the course of the research" (Jennifer Clements, et. al., 1999, p. 34). Researchers are expected to trust that their own natures, (embodied in both their conscious and subconscious minds), the nature of the well designed plan, and the nature of their interactions with participants will germinate and grow into generative knowledge.

The Numinous

For the purpose of its use in an Organic Inquiry, we define *the numinous* as the upperworld counterpart to the chthonic from which the researcher may receive inspiration, direct knowing, and other forms of intersubjective guidance.

The concept of the numinous was not included in the original model for Organic Inquiry, and is solely our addition. We adapted the model with the purpose of balancing the chthonic with the numinous in a quasi-shamanic cosmology (see Figure 1, page 18). We say *quasi*-shamanic because while the fundamental structure of the under-middle-upper worlds of a complete shamanic cosmology are present, this model of Organic Inquiry does not incorporate other elements of what would be considered a whole shamanic model, although future researchers could modify the model to correct further omissions if desired in order to bring the Organic Inquiry model into a full shamanic cosmological construct.

We would strongly recommend taking on such a responsibility with the help of a faculty expert in shamanic studies or an actual practitioner of these sacred arts from a culture where these practices still live in order to avoid inappropriate cultural co-optation of the sacredness inherent in the shamanic worldview, which is still extant as a living philosophy in many societies on the planet today.

Numinous implies a realm of light, creative illumination, or teleological meaningfulness that can also be understood as a realm of higher consciousness. If the numinous realm is viewed as akin to the shamanic upperworld—the time-place in which the researcher meets other guides and teachers (Walsh, 1990, p. 147), and possibly has ecstatic experiences of transformation or knowledge (pp. 147-148)—the numinous can be understood as a necessary part of the Organic model. The guides, teachers, and experiences of transformation that the researcher encounters during an Organic project could take many forms, from supervisors and participants, to the "synchronicities, dreams, intuitions, or other manifestations of inner knowing" (Jennifer Clements et. al., 1998, p. 119) that the methodology founders have located—mistakenly we believe—as solely in the chthonic realm. It is the place where we are sometimes literally taken out of and beyond our mundane personalities into a greater transpersonal reality.

It seems to us that if one includes the chthonic in a model, then the numinous must also be included for the sake of wholism. In an indigenous or participatory cosmology, both the chthonic as lower world and the numinous as upper world would be irreducible, indispensable parts of the whole, and it is the wholism that is sacred.

In our view, the difference between Spirit and the numinous is the difference between embodying or activating energy (Spirit), and background or atmosphere (numinous). For example, a flash of clear, direct knowing that is at once experienced as unarguably authentic and true might be a property of the numinous, whereas the persistent felt sense of a push on the back or a whisper in the ear that seems to carry with it a message or an urge to do something might be an experience of embodied Spirit.

The term *relational* is defined as a type of association discovered by thinking about two or more things at the same time (Webster's, 1976, p. 1916). In Jennifer Clements' use and ours, relational is used to mean the connecting aspects or context between apparently separate or different data in a study, between various ways of knowing, and "between old and new theories, paradigms, cultures, or world views to create a new synthesis" (Neilsen, 1990, p. 28). It is also used to imply the interpersonal or relationship aspects of the study, as are further addressed in Chapters 5 and 8.

Organic Inquiry places a premium on context (Jennifer Clements, et. al., 1998, p. 120), making this methodology particularly useful when investigating phenomena that are essentially relational in arising from the interaction of interpersonal human relationships (in this case usually the relationship between the researchers and the research participants)—for it is the emergent quality of the relationship and the analogy of one thing to another that deepens and enriches knowledge, knowing, and knower.

This aspect of the relational principle thus urges developing relationships with the participants, as appropriate when holding them and their stories as a sacred trust. Conventional researchers might shrink from this development of interpersonal familiarity as introducing researcher bias, as well as bordering on unethical researcher behavior. Researchers using standard methods are expected to not make friends with their subjects. However, it would be a violation of the principles of an Organic Inquiry to maintain a false *power-over* distance between the co-explorers of a topic.

Though we have been speaking here of the relational as it relates to human participants in a study, this is also the area where we are constantly reminded and encouraged to make visible the constant relationship and situation of interdependence with all the forms of life and energy with which we come in contact in the course of our work. If all life is indeed seen as sacred, as in our view this methodology suggests, then it is also of benefit to look beyond the human interactions, and intentionally include the relations with Spirit we will have as we follow this way of knowing.

The Transformative

The word *transformative* we define as a quality of difference that occurs in a shift from one set of assumptions or way of being to another, whereby an essential condition or character of a person is changed in a profound way, which may or may not be lasting.

As the final aspect of the Organic Inquiry principles model, one way *transformative* can be understood is to refer to the process of growing a fully blossomed research project from the seed of one person's experience, a process intended to inspire others to more research on the topic, or with this methodology. Jennifer Clements, et. al. (1999) characterized the transformative aspect this way:

> Both researchers and readers grow by participation in the study so far as they are willing to engage in both the conscious and unconscious aspects of the work and so far as each is willing to be changed by their involvement. To truly experience another's story requires the willingness to be altered by it. A story offers transformation to both the teller and to the listener. Transformation may be an apparently small insight into one's understanding of past actions or it may be a major restructuring of lifestyle. (p. 50)

The section on evaluating knowledge claims further in Chapter 4 addresses transformative learning and transformative changes of heart more fully.

The Natural Growth Metaphor

Our adaptation of the Organic Inquiry model may appear to have more of a quasi-shamanic cosmological structure than the founders of the methodology intended. Their first impulse was to use a natural growth model in which the metaphor of a seed that grows into a fruit tree gives general direction to the research process.

This metaphor has a certain appeal for researchers wanting specifically to link Organic Inquiry with the many traditions of vitalism, or to other study topics that touch on aspects of self-development. There is an implicit rightness in viewing the earth of sacred soil as the lineage of literature into which a study is planted, where the seed is the researchers experiencing of their study topic, the chthonic underground is the unfolding mystery of the unseen course that research takes and the opportunities for patience and trust along the way, the numinous light is the nourishment and guidance that called the seed into being as a research project, and the relational are the participants whose own stories branch off from the researchers' until through its developmental processes the branches bear the fruit of transformative learning and changes of heart.

Just as the principle of transformative growth and eventual harvest completes the life cycle of a tree, it also completes the life cycle of a research project which evolves not only in continuous ways but through many branchings and bifurcations in order to bear the fruit of knowing.

The reconceptualization we have made of the Organic model may be more easily grasped in the quasi-shamanic cosmological structure, as depicted in Figure 1 on page 19

The Sacred

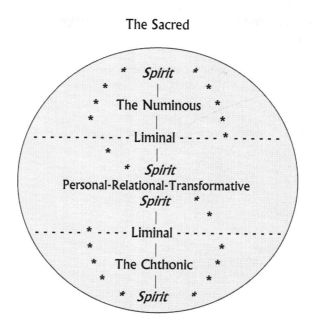

Figure 1. The Adapted Organic Inquiry Cosmological Model

The circle indicates that the sacred embraces all other realms. The dotted lines dividing the interior of the circle into three sections are intended to represent the permeability of the liminal veil, and to illustrate that a liminal veil is positioned between the lower/chthonic and middle/mundane consciousness worlds, and between the middle and upper/numinous worlds. Spirit flows through all three worlds as the inhabiting purposive energy of the sacred. The asterisks flowing as a large letter S represent the energy of Spirit that starts in the middle world, dips down into the chthonic, rises up past the fields of the personal-relational-transformative into the upper world, and descends back to the middle world of human experience. In this way the immanence/transcendence of Spirit is depicted.

Additional Terms Unique to an Organic Inquiry

Liminal

Liminal means in-between, and implies the place/time that exists at the edges shared by consensus reality, and both the chthonic and the numinous realms. It is a unique feature of the revised model of Organic Inquiry (Jennifer Clements, 2000, 2001) that the researchers and the participants are called on to operate in the liminal realm in recalling, gathering, and analyzing data.

We see the liminal as a transition stage to the upper or lower worlds—to the numinous, or to the chthonic of our adapted Organic model. In practical terms, the liminal is a productive transition state reached by shifting consciousness from mundane awareness to an expanded awareness wherein one more easily feels the sacred and hears Spirit, and where the tests and challenges, fears and doubts are reflectively examined. It may also be, at either border, the domain of the trickster (Anderson, 1998, 2000) that brings up self-doubt, or creates transformative (healing) crises, during the research.

Although it may sound as though this shift through the liminal happens in moving from one state to another as a particular event in space/time, in fact it is constantly happening as the researcher moves through the gathering and study of the data. At times it even seems as though the researcher is constantly dwelling in the liminal realm, and this is useful when it happens as it allow the researcher to intentionally see the connections between things that, seen from a more mundane reality, might seem to be very different.

Even though we prefer our adaptation of the original model to Jennifer Clements' revised model, the idea of engaging with the liminal realm is an important part of an Organic Inquiry, one that we incorporated in Deah's dissertation through practices of creating an energetic container for the sacred, and explicitly invoking Spirit into research procedures. However, many other ways of attending to this aspect of an Organic Inquiry are possible, and further explored in Chapter 2.

Spiritual

In contrast to *sacred* which is a quality of being, Spirit*ual* is meant to describe forms of doing; that is, practices that one may do to align with the teleologic energy of Spirit. In this way, we see it as more a verb than a noun. Preparing a meal, for example, could be done within an implicit understanding of the sacredness of always being in communion with the creative and life-nurturing energies of the universe. Specifically giving thanks by prayer or chant to the plant or animal Spirits inhabiting those life forms that now add their life-sustaining and healing energies to the eaters of the meal would be a Spiritual practice.

In our studies, we chose to make the Spiritual the context in which we related both to one another as researcher and associate, but also to the participants in the studies. We even found it necessary to embody this way of relating in all the interactions in our lives, and in doing so, we found it greatly enhanced the quality of our work, and our lives as well.

The Assumptions of an Organic Inquiry

One of the crucial differences that comes into play when considering Organic Inquiry in favor of another methodology is that the Organic approach uses an expanded—and more than cognitive—notion of the self, and makes that notion part of its gestalt throughout. By way of the (adapted) six principles model of the sacred, personal, chthonic, numinous, relational, and transformative as well as the three part process model of engagement with the liminal, Organic Inquiry draws on a concept of the self that is wholistic.

This wholistic concept is one wherein the self is recognized as not necessarily being boundaried by our physical bodies, our personal thoughts and ideas, or even our understandings of who and what we may be. It opens up possibilities of identity and paradigms of possible realities that are beyond the scope of this primer, but that researchers using this methodology should be prepared to encounter and allow themselves to evolve into.

By wholistic, we mean that Organic Inquiry opens the doors to the many subjectivities, using them as appropriate to the topic at hand, so that the rational-analytic mode of generative knowledge is not privileged over the intuitive, somatic, affective, experiential, social, and cultural ways of knowing, and forms of knowledge. As a methodology, and without prescribing specific procedures that could become limiting for researchers, Organic Inquiry clears the way for researchers to use every part of who they are, of who the participants are, as well as what the reader brings, as tools to understand the topic under investigation.

Stimulating transformative change in the researcher(s), the researched, and the eventual reader is an explicit goal of the Organic Inquiry methodology. Transformative change might be viewed as a kind of re-orientation of the self whereby the primary way we have been, and the core understanding we had held about ourselves—whatever these were—are undeniably altered at a root level. With this view of transformative change in mind, allowing and holding the largest possible definitions of self and the nature of reality are essential for the Organic researcher.

Designing a research project to allow—or even encourage—transformative change can be challenging, particularly when transformation is understood to possibly be a profound, lasting, paradigmatic shift. We suggest that it may be more reasonable to understand transformation as including a perceptual shift, or a radical insight, such that one's understanding is altered, or so that obstacles to change are removed so that further transformative changes can later occur. Transformative change might also be understood as that which emancipates experients' attitudes, beliefs, behaviors, or life from the oppressions of shame and fear, allowing them to come out into the warm light of authenticity.

These transformations may be as simple as discovering new ways of relating to the people in one's daily environment, to radically altering one's life pathways, changing careers, moving to a new location, re-evaluating intimate relationships, or awakening new understandings within one's Spiritual life. The possibilities are infinite.

Organic Inquiry has a certain power of sympathetic resonance that connects with the researchers' yearning for a way to explore transpersonal topics that honors the experience under investigation, and does not distort it in order to gain the data of objective science which may carry its own biases. As such it is a living method for exploring and describing lived experiencing, and holds promise for applications to topics hitherto considered unresearchable.

The Limitations of this Methodology

Pitfalls of research arise from an ontology that sees all things as connected, as the Organic methodology does (Dorothy Ettling, 1994). Everything appears not only related, but relevant, and the essential is difficult to distinguish from the meaningfully tangential. The researcher is at risk of both losing focus and simultaneously being uncertain where to set boundaries or make arbitrary selections, thereby including more information than generative knowledge. This distance from the usually expected approaches to qualitative psychological research invites a healthy skepticism regarding the limitations, validity, and significance of such a methodology, prompting a critical question: What is the status of knowledge generated in this way?

To overcome this problem, we recommend including various procedures in the study design that make the research transparent and thereby replicable, and that provide confirmability of findings by way of multiple uses of several interrater strategies. More on this is discussed in Chapter 7.

Special Demands on the Organic Researcher

Operating as if research were a sacred endeavor, and proceeding in partnership with Spirit are no easy tasks. How to do this is left wide open by this methodology's founders, so that persons of all religious and Spiritual affiliations as well as non-believers, can incorporate practices that are meaningful to them.

In our view, upholding these central features of the Organic Inquiry requires the researcher to go beyond conventions and to bring herself or himself into the study in a deeply personal way. Researchers who routinely incorporate Spiritual practices into their lives will have a ready source of processes to drawn on in their research design. Contemplative prayer, meditation, chanting, drumming, or use of sacred texts for guidance could all be used in an Organic Inquiry, as might sacred dance, divination, analytic discourse with Spiritual elders, vision quests, sweat lodge ceremonies, and any of a number of other practices or rituals.

However, it should not be thought that only persons with such experiences or views of reality can use this methodology. All that is really required is to be able to allow one's mind to relax and to allow the possibility that the way the new physics (see Bohm, 1980; Briggs & Peat, 1984; Sheldrake, 1995; Wolf, 1999) posits the interconnectedness of all things—on a quantifiably measurable level—may be true. It is this state of mind, one that allows for this awareness of the interconnectedness of life and the ability to relax one's mind to allow the neurochemicals in the brain to shift into what has been called the relaxation response (Benson, 2000), that are the most essential abilities that will allow anyone to use this approach to research.

Researchers who do not routinely fall into this category and who do not incorporate Spiritual practices into their usual daily routines may find this aspect of an Organic Inquiry challenging, and ultimately transformative. By adopting practices that allow Spiritually-novice researchers to conduct research as if it were sacred and be in partnership with Spirit, researchers open themselves to the possibility that they will be transformed by their own study——which is one of the fervent hopes inherent in an Organic Inquiry. This is not to suggest that Organic Inquiry is some kind of religious conversion experience or that it has a proselytizing agenda. On the contrary, in our view Organic Inquiry embraces the wide diversity of Spiritual and philosophic expressions possible in human experience, and invites researchers to open to and be explicit about whatever resonates for them as sacred.

CHAPTER *2*

The Why

Why Might Research Be a Sacred Endeavor?

In Chapter 1, we discussed the Organic Inquiry model in which the sacred is the essential first principle. We defined the sacred as an attitude or atmosphere in which one is aware of, and respectful and reverential toward, the indwelling of Spirit—which we distinguished as the living energy of *the great mysterious.* We said that to see research as sacred requires that we see ourselves and our interdependence as sacred as well. We now elaborate on this concept of the sacred.

In our view, all of life is sacred. What we mean by that is that there is a larger reality of which we are all a part, and that all parts of this reality are connected. Sometimes this connectedness is visible and obvious, sometimes the connections may not be so readily apparent. Research, as a disciplined way of knowing and creating knowledge, makes explicit the connectedness between individual happenings and universal experience. When the activities of knowing are pursued in an atmosphere of respect for the mysteries of life, and with an attitude of reverence for participants' individual experiences of the unfolding of the topic of investigation in their unique life stories—as an Organic Inquiry does—research can indeed be a sacred endeavor.

We can go even deeper into this understanding of the sacred. As researchers and as human beings we have had experiences that suggest there is a coherent energy flowing through

25

all these disparate parts of reality. Others concur, particularly in the disciplines of frontier physics such as Bohm (1980), Hills (1977), and Tiller (1975, 1999, 2001), and in vitalistic medicine such as Benor (1984, 2001), Kaptchuk (2000), Pierrakos (1990), and Neuberger (1932). For the purposes of our Organic Inquiries, we called this energy *Spirit.* Doing so aligned our view with that of Jennifer Clements (2001) who highlighted the Organic approach to research as not only integrating the sacred, but also in being in partnership with Spirit.

To date, the Organic Inquiry methodology has drawn to itself psychoSpiritually conscious human beings who experientially or intuitively understood the reality of this interconnectedness, and thereby the sacredness, of all life. We (Deah and Steve) held this perspective as the paradigm in which we lived our lives long before discovering the Organic approach to research. When it came time to choose a methodology to study our elusive subject of the experience of healing presence, Organic Inquiry was a clear and logical choice to make.

If as researchers you already believe that all things are sacred and interconnected, you will not be challenged by the tenets of the Organic approach. It does not surprise us to learn that others who hold kindred views of the sacred are similarly drawn to this methodology for human sciences research as Organic Inquiry becomes more well established. For a look how some other Organic researchers have addressed the issues of sacredness and interconnectedness, the reader is referred to the work of Joyce Lounsberry (2001), Carolyn Finn Mitchell (2000), Susan Newton (1996), Rose Anne Pinard (2000), Maja Rode (2000), and Lisa Shields (1996).

For those who hold different beliefs, it might be harder to describe how to understand this concept of interconnectedness. Nonetheless, indigenous ways of knowing and frontier physics have long posited the understanding that all life is interconnected. [see DeQuincey (2000), Kremer, (1999) and Zukav (1980)] For example, it is a physical fact that the atoms that make up the chair you are sitting on might at some future date be transformed by fire or water into other forms. These in time will change yet again. Energy can neither be created nor destroyed. It is clear, even to one who does not believe in our concept of the sacred, that this description is a usable concept.

Our point here is that just as energy can be said to take various forms, and to connect apparently separate things, so too does the sacred. And given that it is the purpose of research to discover and explore unique experiences, find the commonalties among them, and increase not only the certainty of our knowledge claims but also the depth of our understanding of the human condition, we believe that research is inherently a sacred endeavor.

Engaging in Research in a Sacred Manner

Perhaps the more personal question is: why might you, as a novice researcher, elect to engage in research in a sacred manner? To begin to answer that question for yourself, allow us if you will to take you on a gentle journey into the liminal realm——for the best way to get a sense of how Organic Inquiry is different from other approaches to human sciences research is to create (if only in the imagination) an experiential understanding that touches your powers of intuition, feeling, heart, and soul. There are as many ways to travel into the liminal domain as there are stars in the skies, and what we offer here is but one mode to just give a small taste of what it is like.

Journey into the Liminal Domain

First, it is helpful to prepare the mind to relax. You might do this by turning off the phone, putting a *do not disturb* note on your door, playing some meditative music, lighting a candle, and settling comfortably in a chair—-or by making any other preparations that work for you.

Now, begin to relax by closing your eyes, and taking long, slow, deep breaths. Put your attention on how your body feels breathing, just noticing the sensation of chest and belly expanding when you inhale, and noticing the increasing relaxation with each exhale.

When your busy mind presents thoughts to follow, simply re-focus your attention on the sensations of long, deep inhalations, and slow, measured exhalations. If you begin to feel like you are floating, take this as a physiological sign that you are nearing the liminal domain. But don't worry if you don't have this sensation; not everyone experiences this physical sensation of deep relaxation.

When you feel ready, think silently or speak aloud any question you wish regarding doing research in a sacred manner. If you can't think of a question, you might simply hold the intention to imagine seeing yourself engaged in one or more activities during your research that are Spiritual practices for you. The more time you spend doing this, and the more relaxed you become by continuing to breathe in a slow, deep way, the more a variety of ideas will bubble up in your imagination.

If ideas seem to come too fast or change too quickly to be useful, don't worry. Think of this as your subconscious mind sorting through its millions of "files" to present you with the answer you are seeking. Making your question or intention more specific can help to slow down this rapid presentation of information in your imagination.

It is important to allow whatever forms itself in your imagination to be there without judgment. You can decide later whether it is practical or possible within the parameters of your study. For now, just be receptive to whatever is presented to you from the liminal domain.

If one or two images or scenes seem to be holding fairly steady in your imagination, try to notice whether you feel any particular emotional response. Do you feel happy, curious, joyful, sad, fearful? Do you feel a tug at your heart from any image presented? Does you soul dance with joy or in some way resonate with any of the bits of information that come to you in the liminal realm? Paying attention to these kinds of somatosensory responses will help you discern whether a particular option will incorporate well into your research design.

At some point you will either have the answer to your question, or enough options to choose from later, or you will feel that you want to return to this exercise at a better time when you can be more focused and relaxed. It is at this point that you will begin to feel yourself returning to your more normal state of consciousness. I (Deah) find it useful to have pen and paper at hand in order to make notes about the information presented to me on my journey before it slips back into the liminal domain.

To end your journey to the liminal domain, you need only to open your eyes, move your body, and re-engage the critical function of your logical mind.

There are many ways to interact with the liminal domain. What we have suggested above can be done by nearly anyone anywhere with no need for special equipment or fancy instructions. Other practices of specific Spiritual or religious traditions can also be used to engage in research in a sacred manner. The range of options is limited only by the researchers' knowledge, personal comfort, and inclination.

Some Advantages of the Organic Inquiry Methodology

Why might a novice researcher favor the Organic Inquiry approach over other qualitative research methodologies?

The Organic Inquiry methodology is highly flexible, allowing a wide range of data gathering and analysis methods to be tailored for use in an Organic research design. Researchers are free to combine standard methods like interviews and content analysis with more creative processes such as art, dance, poetry, music—just about anything a researcher can think of as a disciplined way to gather and look at participants' stories.

The emphasis on transformative learning—or as Jennifer Clements (2001) posits it, transformative changes of heart and mind—gives immediate benefit to researchers, participants and readers. Researchers stand to be transformed by their participants. Individuals may well gain transformative shifts in their lives or self-understandings from participating in the study. Readers may be touched and inspired to action, while also learning by analogy something life-changing for themselves.

The principle model of Organic Inquiry requires that the :hers brings all of who they are into the study, and invites the ᴊᴀ.... from participants. In this way topics of investigation have increased validity because they are studied from a wholistic perspective.

Organic Inquiry makes explicit the use of various subjectivities as tools for knowing in counterpoint to other methodology's attempts to screen out such essential and introspective lenses. This makes the Organic approach particularly well suited for elusive topics, and ones for which there is no common vocabulary.

Organic Inquiry is fun. For novice researchers who are research-phobic, having a methodology that is so flexible, that insists on allowing researchers to be whole human beings, that values the subjective and the sacred, and that encourages transformations, can make research more of an adventure than an arduous chore.

But is Organic Inquiry right for you? To answer this question, researchers need to know what they want the methodology to do, and in what manner they want to approach their study topic.

The Organic Inquiry methodology intends to produce idiographic knowing. That is, its purpose is to study a topic in rich detail, pursue its uniqueness and subjectivity, and how it is experienced in the life of the study participants. It is particularly well suited as a methodology when researchers have an elusive or ambiguous topic and want to examine it in a careful way, following where the topic and participants lead.

Because of the emphasis on knowing in detail, the semi-structured or unstructured interview methods work nicely in an Organic research design. Interviewing in this way allows researchers to be unconstrained by standardized questions, and to engage in analytic discourse during interviews, though we found that certain broadly focused standardization of questions made sure that participants were addressing a few common points. These interview methods also allow researchers to develop personal relationships with their study participants, making the interview context warm and friendly—which satisfies the Organic principle of the relational.

Jennifer Clements (2001) emphasized developing a group story about the topic under investigation. This might be accomplished in various ways, depending on the researchers preferences and skills. A common method is to include both individual interviews and group inquiry sessions into the research design. Another method is to import the idea of the resonance panel (Anderson, 1998, 2000) into an Organic Inquiry.

Ultimately, we might suggest that the definitive answer as to whether Organic Inquiry is the right methodology for the novice researcher to use will be one's own somatosensory or intuitive response to it. Do you feel a pull in your gut towards it? Does your heart feel filled with joy in the resonance it feels with finding the kind of method you have always dreamed of? Does your mind crackle with barely suppressed energy as you imagine the limitless potentials you can now investigate? If any of these, or similar experiences, are true for you, we would say that Organic Inquiry is a methodology you might want to consider using.

Notes On Chapter 2

One intent of the Organic Inquiry approach to research is to make the final product interactive between the researchers and the readers by way of stimulating transformative changes of heart and mind in the reader. We provide pages or spaces for the novice researcher to make notes about their own projects, as ideas and questions are stimulated by the information we present.

We invite students and their supervising faculty, and other novice researchers to contact us at Publishers@LiminalRealities.com with questions about applications of the methodology.

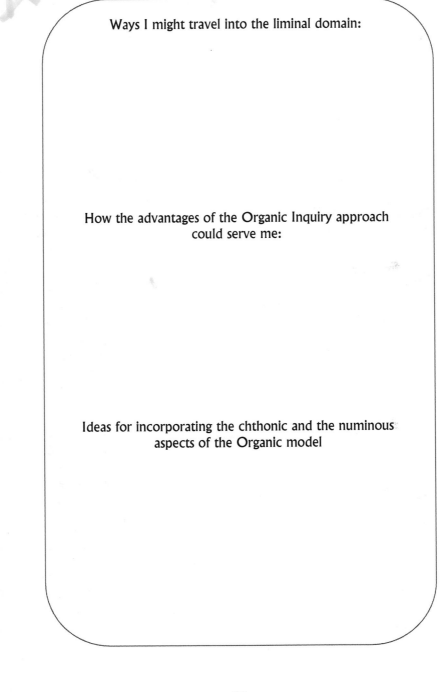

Ways I might travel into the liminal domain:

How the advantages of the Organic Inquiry approach
could serve me:

Ideas for incorporating the chthonic and the numinous
aspects of the Organic model

CHAPTER 3

The Who

Principal Researcher(s)

Just as in other types of novice and student research projects, the research designer is the principal researcher in an Organic Inquiry. It is the principal researcher who is responsible for articulating the formal research question, planning what methods and procedures will be used that will not only answer that question but will also work in harmony with the principles and process models of the Organic Inquiry methodology, and who will be ultimately responsible for all the myriad decisions that are made when a study is underway.

It is the principal researcher who is responsible for recruiting, screening, and scheduling participants; running the study; analyzing the data; and writing the research report—whether that is the summary of findings that is sent to participants, a course or journal paper, a thesis, or dissertation.

The principal researcher is also responsible for ensuring that no harm comes to participants during or as a result of the study. Student researchers will usually submit their research plan for approval by their institutional review board—a body of faculty and others who make sure that a student researcher's proposal conforms to standard guidelines for the protection of human subjects. See the section on institutional review boards further in this chapter for more information on this process.

In an Organic Inquiry, the principal researcher's experiences are also the seed of the research. It is the researchers' interest, passion, or deep questioning that is at least the touchstone of the research study, if not an integral aspect of it. Whether researchers include themselves in their data by going through all the procedures that other study participants will encounter, or instead hold their story outside the data—using it perhaps to illuminate the data through prologue, epilogue, and random interweavings throughout the written report—may be a decision influenced by several factors. The researcher might not be ready to explicate the level of disclosure that is being asked of study participants. A dissertation committee might caution against including personal information. The information might reflect unfavorably on others. The researcher's interest in the topic might not come out of direct personal experience, but rather be prompted by curiosity or indirect observation.

Whether principal researchers include themselves in their research or not, we want to note this point: if pursued as the founders intended, an Organic Inquiry will likely change the researcher in ways that cannot be predicted beforehand. The principle of transformative changes works in—not just through—principal researchers. As with any travel into the liminal domain, where the terrain, inhabitants, and outcome are unknown at the outset, novice researchers may well find that doing an Organic Inquiry becomes an initiation experience.

An initiation figuratively and literally changes you. After you go through the doorway of initiation you are truly another person. Generally you are a more complete person. Parts of yourself you may never have been aware of may come alive and push themselves forward into your new consciousness. You may find that latent talents and abilities now come to you with comfort and ease. Primarily, you will see the world through different eyes, as though through a more carefully focused lens. You are forever changed and you cannot go back to who you were before. Once your eyes are open to this new reality you cannot pretend you do not see what you now see.

If you are open and desirous of this outcome you will find it a blessing. But if you fear change, if you prefer to not take the risk of growing beyond your perceived boundaries, then you may find

34

this initiation a curse. So be aware that what you may now see as simply choosing a research methodology may set you on a new course in your life. Though you may find yourself moved in one direction or another, still it is your choice to accept this movement or not. The opportunities are limitless.

Co-Researchers

Jennifer Clements et. al. (1999) spoke of their research participants as co-researchers as a way to honor the role of others in an exploratory study. This identification makes sense particularly when the primary form of data gathering is the in-depth interview because such a method calls on participants to be self-reflective, which itself is a form of self-study.

Calling participants co-researchers also makes sense when relying on cooperative inquiry groups, where participants have the opportunity to query and respond to each other as part of the cooperative, or collaborative, process of generating data (Heron, 1996).

In my (Deah's) complex study, which used a research associate (Steve), interviewees, and an expert panel that ran in some respects like a cooperative inquiry group, I found it confusing to call all participants co-researchers as this identification blurred the distinctions between the different functions performed by each type of participant—and I found it useful in writing the research report to distinguish between functional types. By maintaining such distinctions, the reader could always be certain to whom I was referring.

Using a research associate as a co-researcher can be particularly beneficial because an Organic Inquiry can generate mountains of data for analysis. Students and novice researchers who have experience with quantitative methods where they used the services of a statistician might view having a research associate as a similar advantage. However, we would like to propose that an even greater use can be made of a research associate as a full fledged co-researcher in an Organic Inquiry.

35

One particular advantage of having a research associate is in being able to double check findings when both principal researcher and research associate are performing the same analysis procedures separately before comparing their results. This increases the trustworthiness of the findings of an Organic Inquiry.

Another advantage of having a co-researcher who is not an interviewee, inquiry group member, nor an expert panel member, is that principal researchers then have a companion and sounding board during the study with whom they can express doubts and worries, brainstorm, and relieve stress when the inevitable unexpected difficulties arise. Researchers and such independent co-researchers—as research associates are—can discuss any and all aspects of the project without compromising the confidentiality and anonymity of the participants.

Some specific guidelines on using a research associate as a co-researcher are outlined in Chapter 8.

Participants

Participants in an Organic Inquiry may take different forms and serve various functions. To a large extent how one wants to gather data will shape some of the criteria that participants must meet. And, how one wants to gather data will be in part influenced by the goals of the study.

In an Organic Inquiry, with its primary focus on investigating a topic in rich detail, and its valuing of storytelling, participants will need to be persons who can articulate their experience of the study topic. For Organic studies in which the interview method is the main data collection procedure, researchers will want to be able to develop rapport with the participants, encourage relevant disclosures, and keep the interview on track.

Some useful resources for developing interviewing skills include:

InterViews: An Introduction to Qualitative Research Interviewing. Steiner Kvale, 1996, Thousand Oaks: Sage Publications.

Qualitative Interviewing: The Art of Hearing Data. Herbert J. Rubin & Irene S. Rubin, 1995, Thousand Oaks: Sage Publications.

The Active Interview. James A. Holstein & Jaber F. Gubrium, Qualitative Research Method Series 37, Thousand Oaks: Sage Publications.

The Vulnerable Observer: Anthropology That Breaks Your Heart. Ruth Behar, 1996, Boston: Beacon Press.

Narrative Knowing and the Human Sciences. Donald E. Polkinghorne, 1988, Albany, NY: SUNY Press.

Research Groups and Expert Panels

The Organic approach also values what Jennifer Clements (2001) referred to as the group story whereby participants interact in some manner with the stories of other participants. In some Organic Inquiries, the group story has been developed as interviewees separately read and respond to vignettes of other interviewees' experiences.

In other studies, the group story is developed in a collaborative context, similar to a Cooperative Inquiry (Heron, 1996), or a Resonance Panel (Anderson, 1998, 2000). More on using participants in an Organic Inquiry can be found in Chapter 7.

While expert panels may be used in an Organic Inquiry, we would caution novice researchers to remember that this approach to research intends to excavate idiographic, or lay, knowledge, and to contribute to the emancipatory goals of the feminist methodologies. Using an expert panel to interpret what lay participants *really* said, or what lay participants' experiences *really* meant, we believe, is out of alignment with the integrity of the tenets of Organic Inquiry. Still, it makes for an interesting layer of findings to incorporate a panel or group inquiry of some kind to add balance and perspective to the data generated through individual interviews. The challenge is in how and when to include a group in the study design, and who will be the group members.

When deciding to use a research group or expert panel a good thing to keep in mind is how will the participants work together. Will members spark each other's responses, or will they compete to monopolize the process? Will members act like a team in pursuing the goals you set for them to accomplish, or will they hijack the process and take the inquiry into unfruitful territory? And can the principal researcher facilitate the group with a light hand, allowing for the unexpected explorations that discover new aspects of the topic under investigation? Obviously selecting the right people is essential.

Because group dynamics and group facilitation can be tricky business, we recommend that novice researchers who are not already skilled facilitators incorporate the group inquiry method into preliminary studies in order to gain experience. Even veteran classroom teachers might do well to think through how their role as a researcher and their role as instructor are different before using a research group as the only data gathering method. For more advice on research groups, the reader is referred to the literature on cooperative inquiry.

Research Site Facility Managers

Where will the participant interviews or group inquiries be held? If at a location such as a university, or a clinic, or some other kind of business place that does not normally rent space for this kind of purpose, researchers will be dealing with the site facility manager. Most of us probably would not consider site facility managers as part of the research team. Nonetheless, these pivotal persons can play a crucial role in the successful management of the research experience. Facility managers are concerned with protecting their clientele or membership, and ensuring that they are not being exploited in any way that would reflect badly on the facility, or create a legal liability for the facility owner.

To start, site facility managers must provide written approval for allowing researchers to use their site, based on your conversation with them, or a summary of your research plan. Their approval letter is then submitted with an institutional review board application.

Managers and others on their staff might be enlisted to help in the recruitment of potential candidates for the study. This works well when the principal researcher has provided clear, simple instructions, and recruitment fliers. It would not generally be advisable to have site managers or staff screen potential study participants, but it is useful to have them point interested persons in your direction.

Sometimes researchers hope to have organizations or associations provide membership lists from which potential research participants can be solicited. In many of these situations the organization's offices would not be used as the research site. Still, approval to recruit from such organizations will require the cooperation of an organizational authority. It is probable that a letter authorizing the use of such an organization's mailing or membership list would also be part of the institutional review board package.

When interviews or group sessions will take place in locations whose primary business it is to rent space for meetings, a site facility manager plays a less important role beyond that of contracting for the use of the space. However, it might be helpful to discuss what other groups would be renting space in nearby rooms, in case any noise or activity you or they might generate would be disturbing to others. In addition, these facility managers may be able to provide simple amenities, such as beverages, snacks, or writing supplies—small touches that the researcher can then not worry about.

Institutional Review Boards

The institutional review board (or IRB) is the entity that approves the researchers' study design at organizations that receive federal funding for research with human participants. They are charged with the responsibility of ensuring that the ethical dimensions of proposed projects have been considered, and that all reasonable and required precautions are taken to protect the mental, emotional, and physical safety of research participants.

Mandated in its current form by the National Research Act in 1974, IRBs came about as an outgrowth of the Nuremberg trials in the aftermath of World War II to prevent atrocities such as those that Nazi scientists perpetrated on mental patients, Jews, homosexuals, gypsies, and other prisoners in the concentration camps. (Heger, 1980).

While different universities and federally funded research institutions may have slightly different ways of interpreting some of the finer points of the IRB regulations, all adhere to three primary principles: (1) protecting participants' autonomy via ensuring the right to fully informed consent, (2) protecting participants' safety by ensuring that the benefits of the project outweigh the risks to participants; and (3) promoting fairness and ethical standards in the recruitment and selection process, and in all study procedures.

IRBs review all proposed protocols, weigh the ethical issues raised, assess potential benefits against possible risks, and assure that appropriate recruitment and consent procedures are used. Most universities have specific guidelines for developing an IRB application that are helpful in expeditiously gaining their approval to start recruiting participants. This is not to say that following the guidelines exactly ensures that the IRB will have no follow up questions or requests of the researcher. This is a normal part of the process and should be expected. Researchers who are operating on a tight timeline will want to factor in potential delays while supplemental application material is prepared for their IRB. Plan in advance to be patient. This is definitely one place where you cannot push the river.

Until Organic Inquiry becomes more well known as a viable research methodology, the novice or student researcher may encounter some difficulties when proposing an Organic design to the institutional review board. By virtue of its innovative position among the range of methodologies commonly used for psychological research, Organic Inquiry challenges conventions on several counts.

The Standard of Anonymity

It makes some IRBs —and some degree committees— nervous to hear that a feminist-oriented research methodology encourages its participants to breach the standard of anonymity by being known by their true names. Their concerns are well-founded. While it might be acceptable to interviewees to be identified authentically, they may—in the course of their interview—mention

40

the names of others who would not wish to be linked to the interview, or to the research. Interviewees may change their minds about their comfort with disclosing some information and regret their decision to release themselves from anonymity. Or, information that is comfortably disclosed at the time of the interview, may in later years turn out to cause an interviewee unforeseen harm, or even simple embarrassment.

Organic Inquiry, nonetheless, encourages researchers to incorporate into the research design opportunities for possible emancipation, and that must include being freed from the oppression of having those in authority decide when one must hide who one is, what one has personally experienced, and when one can be allowed to take full responsibility for oneself.

While some IRBs and some committees may press researchers on these points, I (Deah) found that there are reasonable solutions to at least two of these issues:

1. The names of others mentioned by interviewees can be masked in the conventional way, thus protecting the anonymity of those who had no chance to consent to being even tangentially involved in the project.

2. Direct participants—meaning, interviewees or panel members—can, and should, be given multiple opportunities to change their minds and rescind their decision to be known by their true names. If this occurs, the researcher is then obligated to change all records containing the true name (except the consent form), and substitute a pseudonym. In our opinion, it is in keeping with the tenor of the Organic methodology to allow participants to select their own pseudonym, rather than imposing one on them.

3. Direct participants can be identified by first name only. When the first name is not unusual, there is sufficient protection in the mere fact that it is a common name shared by many. When the first name is readily identifiable, it can be left to the personal judgment of the participant whether to use a pseudonym. While some might argue that using women's first names only contributes to women being viewed on the level of children, we believe that the Organic

41

approach to knowing a subject in rich detail is a casual, friendly, and intimate enough methodology that being on a first name basis is appropriate.

It is the issue of when research participants can be allowed to take full responsibility for their actions, and the consequences—known and unknown—that may encounter the strongest objection from those charged with protecting the subjects in any IRB-approved study. This is, in large part, a philosophic judgment call that brings into question not only the conventions of psychological research, but also the underlying paradigm of paternalism that pervades any hierarchical system. In our studies, we believed this was a point worth fighting for, and it then became incumbent on us to demonstrate to our IRB how we planned to minimize this risk. While the details of minimizing this risk would necessarily change with each proposed research design, some generic factors might apply, such as:

1. wording recruitment materials very carefully to attract persons who are already insistent on taking responsibility for themselves.

2. carefully screening respondents, and including mention of this concern before accepting them into your study.

3. including this philosophical stance in your consent form.

4. when practical, staying in touch with participants after the study has concluded, providing referral information to appropriate helping professionals as needed.

5. giving participants multiple opportunities to use a pseudonym, and documenting that you have done so. Provide these opportunities even years later if using their information for subsequent projects, articles, or releasing your data to other researchers.

Transformative Changes

Some IRBs may stumble over the idea that research can hold as a goal the transformation (i.e. emancipation, in feminist theory terms) of its participants. That Organic Inquiry has as its aim the transformation of heart and mind may be a challenge to the IRB that holds tightly to its function of protecting human subjects, for transformation seems like it might mean crossing the line between doing research and doing therapy.

This is a legitimate concern, and it is helpful to researchers to address this concern up front in their IRB application. We employed two solutions to this initial roadblock. First, we defined transformation of heart and mind as potentially being something as simple as achieving an insight or shifting a point of view. When the emphasis is on a change that bubbles up naturally and spontaneously from within the participant, rather than being imposed on them by something the researcher does or asks them to do, the concept of transformation sounds less risky to an IRB. Second, we spoke more about transformational *learning*—which suggests a non-threatening opening—rather than transformation, which suggests some kind of radical change.

While transformative changes may well happen during an Organic Inquiry, it may be best not to promise this, or even suggest the potential for it in the consent form. Even though it will be a wonderful benefit if it does occur, from the IRB point of view, it is best to allow this to be a delightful unexpected benefit, rather than a potentially unfulfilled promise.

CHAPTER 4

The What and The When

What Do You Want to Know?

Most likely, the topic and your particular passion for it will present to you the general parameters of your research project. If not, one way to hone the topic into a preliminary research question is to have someone ask you what you wish to study, and to keep asking until you find yourself feeling passionate for a particular focus.

Another way might be to play with how many different research questions you can ask yourself that in some way address the six principles of the Organic Inquiry model. For examples:

- What is sacred about the therapeutic alliance?

- How do clients differ in how they experience the sacred in their therapy sessions, or their lives?

- How is the experience of the sacred mediated by personal disclosures in general?

- What is the affective experience of persons who make personal disclosures?

- What is changed in the relationships of persons who make personal disclosures?

- How are relationships changed by experiences of encountering the unknown?

• How are numinous experiences responded to by a specific population?

Any of these questions might spark a passionate interest in a researcher who is curious about sacred experiences, therapy experiences, what different people experience in various settings, etc.

Once the topic of investigation begins to take shape, the formal research question can be formulated.

Formulating Organic Inquiry Research Questions

The purpose of the research question is to focus your investigation by imposing a focusing lens. Even so, in a qualitative study the scope of the question and the investigation may still be quite broad. A typical Organic Inquiry question might be: What is the lived experience of [the topic of investigation], and how does it impact experients? For example, *what is the lived experience of Spiritual connection, and how does feeling Spiritually connected change the experient?*

Alternative phrasings of the Organic research question might be:

What is [subjects'] experience of [topic]?

Example: What is women's experience of using the artistic medium of clay as a Spiritual practice? (Katherine S. McIver, 2001, p. 1)

How might [something thought of one way] be [thought of differently]?

Example: How can life with chronic illness be a better life? (Shirley L. Loffler, 1999, p. 2)

What is the impact of [study topic] on [study participants]?

Example: What is the impact of the Spiritual practice of

46

Tibetan Buddhist guru yoga on the clinical practice of psychotherapy? (Sandra Magnusson, 2001, p. 1)

Organic Inquiry is particularly well suited for exploring concepts that are considered elusive, or overly subjective. Maja A. Rode's (2000) simple question— *What is beauty?*— is an example. Deah's more complex question— *In an environment where clients are seeking healing, how does having a somatosensory experience identified as healing presence impact the experience of healing, what is changed in how clients view their world, and how might this, finally, impact healing?*— illustrates how an Organic research question might be phrased to uncover experiential understandings that are not yet well addressed in any academic literature.

Robin Seeley's (2000) two part question — *What is your vocation and how do you know it; what has been your experience of the process of moving into sacred work at this time in your life?*— exemplifies a research question that invites reflection and discovery for the participant as well as the researcher.

No matter the form, the Organic research question is derived from the fundamental quest to know at least one aspect of a topic in depth, to gain understanding, and to explore the transformative potential of this understanding.

Jennifer Clements (2001) instructed:

One must actually prepare two sets of questions. The first are the questions that motivate the study. What do you want to find out about the topic? The second [set of] questions are given to the participants. The research questions are the foundation for the interview questions. (p. 139)

Novice researchers need to be aware that the phrasing of the research question necessarily imposes a delimiting and pre-conceived lens on the topic. Having any pre-conceived lens in a study that is exploratory and discovery oriented runs the risk of blinding researchers to what will present itself from the data itself, and from the chthonic and numinous realms in an Organic Inquiry. On the other hand, having some delimits on the investigation will be helpful in staying on track and avoiding getting buried under an avalanche of tangential, even if interesting, information.

Part of the art of formulating the research question is to be aware of whether the researcher's biases and assumptions are at play in the wording, and if so, to address these factors as part of the explanation of how the research question has been developed. In an Organic Inquiry, because the researcher's story forms the seed of the research, this background is naturally presented in that context. Some researchers attempt to formulate their question without bias and assumption. We suggest that this is difficult if not impossible to achieve because every question lives within a context of some kind, and every context is inhabited by its own conscious or unconscious biases and assumptions.

Even the elegantly simple question of *What is beauty* assumes that beauty is something, and that that something can be articulated and explored. The bias in this question is in the use of the word *what.* Rode's bias appears to be that beauty is a thing. Consider the difference had she phrased her question differently: *how* is beauty might suggest a bias that beauty is a process, or *when* is beauty, might imply that beauty is a temporal experience. Each tiny word change shifts the entire focus of investigation.

When to Choose This Methodology

In summary, we believe the time to choose the Organic Inquiry methodology is when the researcher wants to explore an experiential topic in an experiential, intuitive, affective, analytical and disciplined way. The time is also when there is a readiness within the researcher to take some risks in their own lives, though this may not be something one will be aware of at the time. If this methodology is right for someone, they will know it is. It will feel like it is time to do it - in *this* way for *these* reasons, whatever they may be for each individual.

Though we have made a point of emphasizing that anyone could do Organic Inquiry—and this is true—in reality it is likely that only those who have a burning desire to explore extraordinary topics using a cutting edge methodology will be the ones who actually choose to do so. We believe it takes a certain kind of person, at a certain point in their lives to take on the rigors of an Organic Inquiry. One must have a strong commitment to embodying Spirit into one's life, as the brave soul choosing this route will receive considerable resistance at times from all quarters, with supporters coming few and far between. One must be willing to take the risk that one will be challenged by one's fellow researchers, fellow students, and perhaps even by one's own faculty and advisers.

In our opinion one will choose this methodology when one is ready to significantly change one's own life, and to stand with those who have chosen to bring a new way of doing research – as though it were sacred – into being. It is an exciting and challenging path to choose, and one that will bring greater and more unexpected rewards than might be imagined when one begins. Choose wisely and, as Organic Inquiry proposes, things will work out as they are meant to.

Notes on Chapter 4

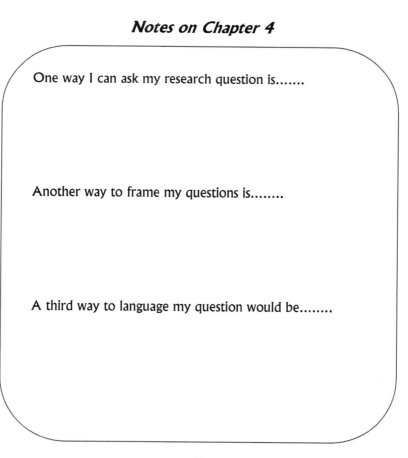

One way I can ask my research question is.......

Another way to frame my questions is........

A third way to language my question would be........

Which question form gives me the best framework
for my study?

How will the principles and processes of Organic Inquiry
help me answer my research question?

CHAPTER 5

🍃

Evaluating Knowledge Claims
in an Organic Inquiry

The unique features of the Organic Inquiry methodology challenge the normative views of validity in research. This section briefly identifies those challenges, and enumerates one way knowledge claims can be evaluated in the Organic study. Several expanded views on validity are offered from clinical, health, and transpersonal psychology, including a four-part model of validity developed by Maja A. Rode (2000) for another Organic Inquiry.

Challenges to the Normative View of Validity

In reviewing various epistemological and ontological paradigms for their relevance to the development of the field of health psychology, Lyons (1999) wrote:

> Concepts such as reliability, validity and generalizability are often irrelevant in the evaluation of qualitative research as they are based on assumptions central to a positivist perspective....Evaluation criteria depend on the epistemological assumptions of the particular research paradigm...so any evaluation questions must take into account the paradigm within which the research was carried out. (pp. 247-248)

Taking Lyon's perspective, evaluation criteria for an Organic Inquiry arise from the cosmological and ontological assumptions of the methodology, and from the epistemological assumptions embedded in the subjectivities of idiographic and experiential ways of knowing. The sort of validity that strives for positivist certainty, or relies on quantitative measurement is irrelevant to an Organic study that seeks to paint a richly descriptive picture of a specific experience.

Reviewing issues of validity in qualitative research for medicine, Malterud (1993, 2001) advanced a view of validity that is a "systematic and reflective process for development of knowledge that can somehow be contested and shared, implying ambitions of transferability beyond the study setting" (p. 2). She advocated adding the notion of reflexivity to evaluation of qualitative research so that researchers' background, and biases can be visible (p. 3). Hall and Calley (2001) supported the ideas of "reflexivity, which addresses the influence of investigator-participant interactions on the research process, and relationality, which addresses power and trust relationships between participants and researchers, hav[ing] the potential to increase the validity of the findings..." (p. 2) We advocate adding these considerations to an expanded view of validity for an Organic Inquiry.

Creswell (1994) claimed that "qualitative researchers have no single stance or consensus on addressing traditional topics such as validity and reliability in qualitative studies" (p. 157). He found it useful in research proposals to discuss accuracy of information, generalizability of findings, and reliability limitations for replication. Accuracy can be pursued through participants' reviews of the vignettes drawn from their interviews and from other comments and feedback on your interpretation of their experience; through triangulating analytic impressions between participants individually, research associate (if used) and researcher, and participant group or expert panel; and through presenting careful data analysis audit trails.

Generalizability may be limited in Organic Inquiries when the research is confined to a specific context, although this limitation does not necessarily curtail the potential for developing generative knowledge. Transparency of process and researcher reflexivity may serve others who attempt to replicate an Organic study with different data gathering and analysis methods. Creswell's view points to the need to specify the criteria so that the research can be designed to meet its own declared standards, as this will help readers understand its usefulness.

Writing from a feminist perspective, Dallimore (2000) argued that validity comes from using a variety of methods that "allow researchers to capture the experiences of participants using participants' own voices" (p. 2) and by overt attempts to garner relationships with research participants, instead of the conventional strategy of holding oneself distant from the participants. Likewise, Acker, Barry, and Esseveld (1991) suggested that not only should the participants' voices be heard, but also that the investigator should be visible in interpretations of the research (p. 145).

Ussher (1999) reminded feminist health researchers that *lay knowledge*—that is, uninterpreted participant voices—is open to the same scrutiny for credibility as is *expert*—presumably researcher analyzed, interpreted, and critiqued—knowledge. Nonetheless, she also pointed out that a feminist standpoint epistemology, in which Organic Inquiry could be included, legitimately emphasizes the "role of research as an impetus for social change, and encourages the use of the research process for empowerment, through a focus on women's agency and by providing new accounts of women's experience" (p. 110). We advocate adding these considerations as well to an expanded view of validity for an Organic Inquiry.

Dallimore also suggested that a strategy of collaboration with participants in developing, analyzing, and interpreting data increases trustworthiness of the results (p. 7). We would add that collaboration does not have to mean group process. Participants can individually collaborate with the researcher on clarifying the meaning of their statements about their experience, and they can collaborate with the researcher in critical and analytic discourse without such interaction occurring in a group meeting.

Collaboration can also happen between researcher and research associate as you work together to elicit the essential description of the study topic from the data, and to develop a synthesis statement about it that reflects both the experience and the validity or trustworthiness of the reports about the experience. In fact, this is one of the principle advantages to having a research associate.

"Another possible means by which feminist researchers could demonstrate the validity of their findings is through using those findings to achieve their goals of emancipating and creating change for women" (Dallimore, p. 9). At the risk of alienating feminist purists, we suggest that women are not the only segment of postmodern society who benefit from movement towards emancipation from oppression. The modernist worldview and the positivist scientific method oppress all researchers in the sense of restricting some options for inquiry, and impact all persons whose lives and choices are constrained by these other-constructed views of their experience. The Organic Inquiry goal of transformative changes of heart applies not only to the participants in a study, but also to the users of the research in the applicable disciplines to which the study pertains, as well as to the eventual readers of the work.

Heron (1996), an advocate of a collaborative style of inquiry, preferred to reclaim the term *validity* for qualitative social science research, applying to it a different meaning from the conventional idea that a procedure or study has validity when it can be guaranteed to measure what it purports to measure. Heron asserted that "research findings are valid if they are sound or well-grounded, and have been reached by a...reasoned way of grounding them" (p. 159). What is sound is determined by whether the finding is in "wholesome relation" (p. 159) to the cosmological, ontological, and epistemological constructs from which the research design, and the researcher proceed.

This type of validity calls for the researcher's integrity and critical thinking to be visible in every step of the process so that others can see that the wholesome relationships the researcher finds in the data are supported not only by the literature but also by the paradigmatic assumptions underlying the methodology. We advocate adding these considerations to an expanded view of validity for an Organic Inquiry, also.

The Spiritual nature of Organic Inquiry sharply calls into question how we know what we know, and what we will allow to be called knowledge. As a transpersonal methodology, it overtly pushes at the edges of the experiential and the Spiritual as tools of knowing as well as phenomena to be known. As a feminist approach, it intentionally revises the relationship between the researched and the researcher to acknowledge and employ the mutuality of co-investigation of lived experience.

As such, Organic Inquiry may make the more conventional and seasoned researcher apprehensive about the validity, credibility, generalizability, or reliability of the organic knowledge claim. Further confounding the norms of validity is the fact that the methodology calls for asking for Spirit to guide the endeavor, trusting where Spirit leads, surrendering to the process, and recognizing when the inquiry has reached a plateau of for-the-moment completeness. In feminist fashion, this approach seeks to emancipate the art and science of research from the dictates of other methods by giving more freedom of movement to the researcher, and allowing the participants' stories to speak for themselves.

Still, the question of research validity is of paramount importance even though these considerations have been reframed by some qualitative researchers such as Braud (1998), Giorgi (1989), Heron (1996), Packer and Addison (1989), Maja A. Rode (2000), Smith (2000), Ussher (1999), and Van Manen (1990), to name a few. Overall, the basic concern for trustworthiness in research still applies. In qualitative, and especially in descriptive and interpretive research, as Packer and Addison pointed out, "truth is seen as an ongoing and unfolding process, where each successive interpretation has the possibility of uncovering or opening up new possibilities" (p. 56).

From the conventional perspective, Organic Inquiry in its original model as a methodology could be charged with lacking scientific rigor because of its under-developed consideration of the issues of trustworthiness. Braud (1998) held that validity has to do with more than intellect alone, that the faculties of bodily wisdom, emotion and feeling responses, intuition and instinct, tacit knowing, experiential adequacy, coherence or consensus, and sympathetic resonance (pp. 214-226) contribute to the trustworthiness of knowledge claims.

The Organic method expects the research, the researchers, and the readers to open to the sacred, to an expanded consciousness in order to deepen and enliven the knowing and the known (Jennifer Clements et. al., 1998, p. 117). It holds the products of intellect (mental analysis) up to the responses of body, emotions, intuition, liminal realm (subconscious), and to alignment (resonance) with others (consensus), with past and present experience (experiential adequacy). In so doing, it requires us to view validity differently.

Maja A. Rode (2000), in her dissertation using the Organic approach, suggested considering four types of validity that she identified as objective, subjective, transformative, and the self-evident. Objective validity—also called verification by Maja Rode (pp. 101-102)—in a predominantly narrative method like Organic Inquiry occurs when participants review the transcripts or vignettes of their stories from which further analysis is to be derived. By revising the portrayal of their experience, participants are providing an objective validity: "This is what I said, this is what I meant, this verbal description matches my somatic experience." Verification is also provided through the discernment of the researcher in recognizing the participants' stories as of the same logical type as her own (Maja A. Rode, p. 102). We have used this kind of discernment throughout analysis procedures and during recruitment screening, during interviewing, and during the altaring (indwelling) time of the analysis procedures.

Subjective validity, Maja Rode (2000) would say, becomes the result of researchers' and participants' independent and interdependent ability to exercise self-reflective observation. At some level, all knowledge is subjective because we can only know what we have the capacity to know, and that capacity is shaped by a myriad of interactive factors.

For example, in Deah's pilot study one participant arrived for an experiential creative arts session immediately after having dental work done. By her own admission, at the beginning of the session her attention was not fully engaged with the research task of recalling a vivid experience of healing presence. Her capacity to access her memory of her experience of the topic under investigation was impacted by the invasive nature of dental work, and her consciousness was altered by the lingering sound of the cleaning tools.

Through discussion of how she felt disconnected and shut off as a defense against the invasion of dentistry, her experience of herself began to shift, and she commented on feeling an increased capacity to be present to her surroundings, to Deah, to the conversation, to the instructions for the research task, and, most importantly, to her embodied memory. This participant's remembered experience became filtered through her lived-experiences of the day of research, giving her creative expression represented in clay a heightened subjective validity because the exercise of working with the clay reproduced an in-the-moment experience while also accessing a visual and somatic memory of past experiences. One experience validated the other, and both were validated in her subjective—that is, internally referent—and experiential way of knowing.

Self-evident validity is derived from awareness of direct experience (Maja Rode, 2000, p. 105). That is, we can have experiential knowledge of the beauty, sheer awe, and healing quality of the purple-rose-orange clouds of sunset against a jagged and snowcapped mountain range without needing to understanding atmospheric conditions, the physics of light, or the physiology of the optic nerve. Through our experiencing of the sunset, we come to know its beauty. Something within us resonates to the experience, and confirms our knowledge. Maja Rode wrote:

> ...simply be aware of what is—without needing to conceptualize, categorize, analyze, grasp, prove, or define. We have forgotten that any analysis or understanding is always at least a step removed from the simple self-evident truth that lies before us. Do you see beauty in a rose? That is what beauty is. Do you want to know sweetness? Taste this sugar. (p. 105)

Phelon (2001) in her dissertation on therapists' experience of healing presence, used self-evident confirmation as a recruitment screening criteria: Persons who intuitively understood what she meant by the term *presence* were selected as participants for her study. The word resonated with something within them, and gave a self-evident validation about their usefulness as research participants.

In a similar manner, participants in Deah's study also used self-evident validity when they responded to recruitment fliers. They recognized themselves in the call for persons who had had experience of healing presence with a naturopathic physician even before Deah gave a preliminary definition of healing presence. No one who responded during the recruitment phase of the project misunderstood the term *healing presence*.

It is Maja Rode's (2000) concept of transformational validity—what Jennifer Clements (2001) would call transformative changes of heart (p. 65)—that is of special concern to any Organic Inquiry project because the primary goal of the approach is transformation. Transformational validity asks of the research: to what extent do the participants' stories inspire the reader, and to what degree has embracing the sacred and partnering with Spirit made a difference in what we have learned about this phenomenon, and about the processes of research?

Maja Rode suggested that "the measure of validity is...related to the degree of transformation resulting from the research conducted and communicated....[She saw] transformation as an internal evolution that is externally expressed" (p. 104). She offered as examples of such validity "a deepened capacity to love, a greater sense of connectivity, less fear, or greater self-acceptance" (p. 104). Movement from an interior experience of such transformation to an exterior expression or change in one's way of being is a second order change, and such shift may be seen in interviewees as interviews unfold.

Maja Rode concluded that the transformative validity of an Organic Inquiry can only be assessed by the individual reader, because "it rests on the sincerity, honesty, and curiosity that you bring to your own exploration of the topic" (p. 104). In other words, if a study has transformative validity, the reader who comes to it with an open mind and receptive Spirit will be changed or inspired by it.

Some may ask whether a study that produces no transformative changes of mind or heart can still be considered an Organic Inquiry. We would say that yes, it can. Transformative insights and shifts in how one relates to self, to Spirit, and to one's community may be placed on a continuum that ranges from small bifurcations such as learning that using meta-verbal expressive arts activities in research, for example, may yield valuable information that can be gained in no other way, to life-altering shifts in self-concept, in ability and willingness to surrender to a partnership with Spirit, or to a change in values that incorporate service to one's community.

Part of partnering with Spirit, in our opinion, is trusting in the idea of sacred timing. That is, transformations do not have to occur within the timeframe of a research project. They may not occur until after years have elapsed and some new experience connects with the memory of participating in the research, at which point researcher, participants, or readers may have an "aha" upon which to base a transformative change in their life. An Organic Inquiry plants the seed, but in the larger context of participants' lives, they must provide the water and the sun for growthful meaning in their own gardens of transformation.

Jennifer Clements (2001) wrote that "a study has transformative validity when it succeeds in affecting the individual reader through identification with and change of the prevailing story [of one's own life]...the validity of research that inspires transformative change must depend on the individual experience of the individual reader" (p. 217). Jennifer Clements cautioned that in an Organic Inquiry the burden for accurately using effective procedures may be even more necessary than in other methodologies because the data sources and the analysis procedures are highly "subjective and Spiritual" (p. 218). She added to the aforementioned views on validity a call for discernment, particularly in regard to making explicit aspects of the sacred and the involvement of Spirit in research.

> One must combine what is objective with what is subjective, and be clear about which is which....Spiritual influence offers both confirmation and also the opportunity for self-delusion...We must examine our experience and our motives once, and then again, to be clear about their meaning and their implications and then...report extensively on our procedures and experiences so that the reader may agree or disagree. (pp. 219-220)

Ferrer (2002) argued that the inner empiricism that transpersonal theory has adopted—summarized as "transpersonal and Spiritual knowledge claims are valid because they can be replicated and tested through disciplined introspection, and can therefore be intersubjectively verified or falsified" (pp. 42-43)— while having several proponents (Anderson, 1998, 2000; Maslow, 1970; Nagata, 2000; Rothberg, 1994; Tart, 1971, 1977, 1983; Washburn, 1995; Wilbur, 1990) is fatally flawed for several reasons. Such inner empiricism perpetuates the fragmentation of knowledge, knowing, and knower. It insists on a correspondence notion of "reality" where an interior experience is considered "real" only when there are biochemical or physiological functions or structures to account for it. And, it privileges the dominance of objectivity over all other ways of knowing. Instead, Ferrer argued for a transformative validity for Spiritual knowing:

> As for the thorny issue of the validity of Spiritual insights, I should say that the criteria stemming from a participatory account of Spiritual knowing can no longer be simply dependent on the picture of reality disclosed...but on the kind of transformation of self, community, and world facilitated by their enaction and expression. That is, once we fully accept the creative link between human beings and the real in Spiritual knowing, judgments about how accurately Spiritual claims correspond to or represent ultimate reality become nearly meaningless. (p. 167)

Echoing Ferrer's position on transpersonal theory, Kremer suggested that when Organic Inquiry is viewed alternatively from a discourse model of truth, the nature of the methodology can be conceptualized in a broader way:

> What Organic Inquiry really is, is an elaborate way of contextualizing an explicitly differentiated subjectivity (Spiritual to somatic) by connecting it through a certain defined procedure with other subjectivities and using discourse, conversation, art, etc., as ways of resolving issues of reliability, bias, validity....[In this view] the procedure is transparent and replicable... (J. Kremer, personal communication, February 14, 2002)

From these several perspectives, then, we have seen that in health psychology, feminist, and transpersonal research the question of validity can be variously framed. What remains constant is the concern for producing meaningful information that has the potential for utility beyond the context of the participants involved in a specific study.

Whether we adopt or adapt the term *validity*, and its usual companions—reliability and generalizability—the researcher cannot escape the need to conduct a study with some kind of evaluation criteria in mind. We have drawn on health psychology, feminist, cooperative, and transpersonal inquiry ideas on validity in particular because the topic we investigated has elements of each of these domains. Other researchers may want to consider concepts of validity as drawn from other disciplines more closely aligned with their own study topic.

n claiming the lineages of transpersonal and feminist theory, the Organic Inquiry approach benefits from considering the idea of validity from within these perspectives as well. Still, it remains to operationalize these different views of validity and reliability into a working set of standards and criteria for the Organic Inquiry.

Suggested Evaluation Standards and Criteria

The emerging transpersonal approaches to validity (Anderson, 1998, 2000; Braud, 1998; Ferrer, 2002)—with their emphasis on the trustworthiness of expanded ways of knowing, somatic resonance, and embodied and expressed transformative change—fit both the Organic methodology and many topics that novice researchers might explore.

Implicit in the way we frame the Organic Inquiry approach are evaluation standards of reflexivity, relationality, transformational learning and transformative changes of heart, Spiritual engagement, and sacred embodiment. Each of these standards implies certain criteria, which then suggest specific procedures for each study. In explaining these relationships, we return to the six principles of the adapted Organic Inquiry model: the sacred, the chthonic, the numinous, the personal, the relational, and the transformative.

Reflexivity

The standard of reflexivity not only contributes to validity in an Organic Inquiry, but it also addresses the Organic principle of the personal. Reflexivity calls for the researcher to use the seed of her or his own experience to germinate the research project. Through the study, the researcher generates what others have called an audit trail, and what we called the reflective process journal. Through recording and reporting dilemmas and decisions throughout the project, not only do researchers have a way to catch self-delusions and bias, but also readers are able to more clearly see errors in judgment.

The reflective process journal also serves to track when the research design shifts to accommodate new learnings or considerations as they arise in order to enrich the investigation. And most importantly, it records the interactions between researcher and research associate (or between student researcher and committee) as collaboration and consultation occur on data analysis and other aspects of the study.

The criteria for evaluating reflexivity is in how transparent the research processes are, and how clear are the steps for replication. If another novice researcher can follow what has been done, understand process decisions and be guided by them, or review the several data analysis procedures used and arrive at the same general conclusions, then the standard of reflexivity is met. If researcher assumptions and biases have been outlined such that the reader can understand what colors your viewpoints and interpretations, then the standard of reflexivity is further met.

Principal researchers working with co-researchers may find another aspect of reflexivity emerging in an Organic Inquiry—that of how researchers work together, and how their relationship is safeguarded during the stresses of the work. For us, the ultimate standard of reflexivity was the intimate interaction between us. We were in contact on an almost daily basis, and often several times a day. To be specific, we made the health of our relationship and our personal health the priority over the research and over the dissertation ultimately stemming from it. We actually changed the way we worked on several occasions to satisfy this priority and found that, not only did the quality of our work not suffer, it improved significantly. This example of *living the method* cannot be over-stated. We feel maintaining the personal health of all participants is of paramount importance.

Relationality

The standard of relationality not only increases reliability in an Organic Inquiry due to the triangulation of the various participants, it also increases the mutuality of the researcher-participant interaction, placing the study in the feminist tradition in research while also addressing the Organic principle of the relational. Care should be taken during the interviews to create rapport, invite critical reflection, and to join and move with the interviewees in mutual empathy and engender a sense of empathic attunement. Researchers should engage interviewees as co-explorers of the topic under investigation, and co-developers of a rich description of how that experience moves in their lives.

The strictly bound researcher role that requires separateness and distance inhibits the mutuality of discovery in a dialogic process, and violates the relationality of the feminist tenets of Organic Inquiry. Even so, it is crucial to remember that there are some important role differences between primary investigator and participants. The research necessarily reflects the researcher's understanding of the commonalties of participants' experiences, the essential characteristics of the experience and the participants, and how the findings of the research fit into the grounding literatures of the topic. Role relationships can be shaped such that the researcher alone ultimately makes the hard decisions and distinctions, even though this is done after relationship-valuing collaboration takes all viewpoints into account.

The criteria for evaluating relationality is in how well the parts depict or support the whole, and how much empathic attunement is achieved between researcher and participants. Whether the parts depict or support the whole and whether empathic attunement is achieved can be seen when products of analysis are compared to interviewee transcripts and vignettes, and in other checks on findings. That empathic attunement is achieved might also be seen in comments from the reflective process journal.

Transformative Learning and Transformative Changes of Heart

The paired standards of transformational learning (insight, or shift in assumptions) and transformative changes of heart (shifts to egolessness, or inspired acts of compassion) expand and clarify the Organic principle of the transformative, and set it within the feminist tradition, as well as the participatory ontology revision of transpersonal theory. For Jennifer Clements (2001), the aspect of the transformative is the goal of an Organic Inquiry, the harvesting of the fruits of the research. While it is framed as the hoped for outcome that the ultimate reader will achieve, we suggest that both transformational learning and transformative changes of heart can occur all along the way to all participants, including the researchers.

The criteria for evaluating transformative learning for participants can be in the insights that occur during interviews and in follow-ups to any other data gathering procedures. We recommend that researchers include in the research design some way to gather feedback from participants on the experience of being in the study so that this important aspect of an Organic Inquiry is not forgotten.

Researchers might also include in the research protocols some way to notice when you also experience transformative learning or transformative changes of heart during your project. The criteria for evaluating these transformative shifts can then be noted in your comments in the discussion chapter or section of your report.

Spiritual Engagement

The standard of Spiritual engagement is pivotal in an Organic Inquiry, and addresses the paired principles of the chthonic and the numinous in our adaptation of the Organic model. It is the expectation of an Organic Inquiry that the researcher will partner with Spirit. If the participants also partner with Spirit, this is a bonus, although for some projects it may not be required.

Partnering with Spirit means not only being open to Spiritual knowing (Ferrer, 2002) that comes from "traveling to the liminal" (Jennifer Clements, 2000) and confronting the tricksters (Anderson, 1998, 2000) that may make themselves known there, but also explicating knowledge from the chthonic (the unconscious), and accepting guidance from the numinous by way of the various forms that teachers can take, such as research participants, supervisors, strangers ostensibly not involved with the project, or environmental qi (or energy) and other bodily-felt resonances. To partner with Spirit means to be open to the paths for investigation that Spirit energetically prompts one to take, and to attend to the many forms of direct knowing by which Spirit communicates, such as intuitive hunches, flashes of inspiration and creativity, or the felt sense (Gendlin, 1978, 1997) to name but a few.

The criteria for evaluation of Spiritual engagement include listening to or following Spiritual guidance, and in using procedures that explicitly invite Spiritual guidance into interactions with participants, and into the data analysis and interpretation. One example of listening to and following Spiritual guidance that Deah used in her pilot study was her ability to access the liminal portal to the numinous with a simple centering breath, and intention to get her cognitive mind out of the way and allow Spirit to speak through the mode of direct knowing that comes with being in a slightly altered, and more open state of consciousness. Steve and Deah both used this simple procedure when engaging with interviewees' stories in research projects.

Sacred Embodiment

The standard of sacred embodiment is fundamental in an Organic Inquiry, and addresses the principle of the sacred. We conceptualize the sacred as an atmosphere and an attitude. It is the atmosphere in which all research procedures take place, and it is the attitude of reverence and respect with which to hold participants and processes, and the grounding literature for the study.

For the sacred to be truly present in a research project, and because the researcher's mind can become overly focused on the linear, cognitive tasks at hand, it is useful to accept a trusting posture: embody the sacred by interacting with reverence and respect, and trust that all was unfolding as it should be. That is, in the study embodying the sacred might mean that you do your part in logically organizing and carefully administering the research design, and cognitively preparing yourself through your knowledge of the literature. And then, surrender with love and in trust to the "Mystery of being in which we creatively participate" (Ferrer, 2002, p. 134) and through which we are all connected.

The criteria for evaluation of sacred embodiment can be reflected in various of researcher's design elements. We like to create an energetic container for the sacred by enacting personal rituals that shift consciousness from the mundane to the sacred-embodied. We also think of the time spent absorbing and fully understanding the interviewees' stories as *altaring* the transcripts—that is, taking their experience to the altar, or what Moustakas (1990) called *indwelling* the participants' stories until a deep and whole understanding of their experience is attained.

Sacred embodiment is also represented in comments from the reflective process journal as moments of reverence, respect, love, trust, surrender, and connectedness experienced as gifts from the Mystery of being. A further criteria for the evaluation of sacred embodiment is in the extent to which participants notice within themselves a sense of the sacred during their interactions with the research procedures, and or have an unexpected sense of recognition or connectedness from reading the synthesis statements.

Some Final Points in Considering Validity

Anderson (1998, 2000), uses a principle of sympathetic resonance to "reconceptualize and re-enchant validity" (2000, p. 32). She wrote that "...the validity of findings is...formed through consensus building that notes consonance, dissonance, or neutrality..." (p. 33). Braud (1998) also advocated seeking coherence to confirm validity. Braud pointed out that validity is a way of valuing, and that we are making value judgments, explicitly and implicitly all the time anyway.

We contend that incorporating experiential modes of validity into the research design, and then testing them with structured (if not standardized) processes provides procedures for validity that ensure the trustworthiness of an organic inquiry. Some experiential modes of validity might include: bodily wisdom, emotions, aesthetic feelings and direct knowing (Braud, 1998); the senses of resonance, coherence, and dissonance (Anderson, 2000); and interview craftsmanship, dialogic communication, and pragmatic effectiveness (Kvale, 1996).

Braud (1998) further suggested using bodily-felt resonance as "an indicator of fullness and fidelity...therefore...of validity" (p. 224), while noting impedances, described as "the various filters or resistances that might exist...and might interfere with the faithful reception, processing, or expression of the essence of an experience" (p. 227). This somatic awareness validity check serves well to confirm bodily-centered subjectivities, and is particularly consistent with investigations of somatosensory and other elusive phenomena as it is an instrument of the same logical type as the experience under investigation, thereby increasing the trustworthiness of the findings.

Anderson's (2000) resonance panels could be viewed as successive cooperative inquiry (Heron, 1996) groups with a special mandate not to develop data, but to "modify and refine the common themes" (Anderson, p. 37) found in prior data analysis and by preceding panels of diverse cultural groups, thereby providing a more generalizable reliability to the final version of findings. Although Anderson does not use the term *impedance*, she relies on processes that seek consonance, dissonance and neutrality in holding findings up to somato-cognitive resonance. Thus the embodied mind becomes an instrument for confirmation or disconfirmation of reliability.

In summary, the need for standards and criteria of validity is still beginning to be explicated in the Organic Inquiry approach to research. Organic studies may yield more depth than breadth, and findings do not necessarily transfer to a larger population or a different context. As a whole, an Organic Inquiry is likely to be viewed as unorthodox even among those who favor qualitative research.

However, on a developmental note, it seems necessary—if new research methodologies are to emerge onto the landscape of the postmodern quest not just for knowledge but for deep understanding—that early studies using these methodologies also serve to grow the construction of new theories and applications of inquiry. Objections raised by critics and adaptations made by proponents serve to identify weaknesses, and build on strengths. It is our intention to do both in this primer for novice researchers.

Notes on Chapter 5

What validity concerns do I have for my project?

What standards for evaluation will I apply to my study?

How will I incorporate various subjectivities
as ways of knowing in my study?

CHAPTER 6

COMPARING SEVERAL ANALYSIS METHODS

Having used Organic Inquiry as our methodology in three research projects, we can offer some discussion about how the data analysis expectations of this methodology might provide better guidance for novice researchers in making knowledge claims as well as reporting on transformative changes of heart and mind.

Evaluation of Some Data Analysis Procedures

In searching for some detailed analysis steps that would be consistent with Organic Inquiry in general, and that would be appropriate for our research goals in particular, we have evaluated interview analysis, narrative analysis, sequential analysis, heuristic analysis, and intuitive inquiry to determine which of these approaches would serve our specific research purposes as well as enrich the Organic Inquiry methodology. Novice researchers might find a similar preliminary comparison worth the time in order to decide which data analysis method will not only answer the research question posed, but also be manageable to use.

The interpretive interview method was tested because we were completely unfamiliar with such an approach. An evaluation is presented in the section on Kvale's options further in this chapter. The sequential method was tested because we wanted to compare it to a procedure we had spontaneously crafted in an earlier project.

An evaluation is given in the section on Miles and Huberman's suggestions for analysis. A test-study participant used a feedback process based on the Organic procedure of participant analysis, as gleaned from Jennifer Clements' (2001; and Jennifer Clements, et. al. 1999) writings. An evaluation of participant analysis is given later in this chapter.

It should be noted that in evaluating these procedures, we had some particular questions in mind that fit our specific research question. Other researchers seeking the best analysis method for their studies might want to use different evaluation criteria. Of each analysis method, we asked:

1. Does this procedure resonate with the tone and tenets of Organic Inquiry, especially the sacred and transformative features?

2. Will this procedure help us answer the general research question?

3. Would participants be able, and likely to be willing, to use this procedure to analyze their own transcript and others?

4. What might happen to the study if the analysis method is too complicated for participants to use consistently?

5. Will the procedure generate rich and meaningful description without overwhelming us in tangential detail? Will it help us distinguish between essential data and tangential information?

6. Will the procedure be satisfying to follow (i.e., does it resonate with our own styles of working, does it fit with our intended use of intuition, and somatosensory knowing)? Will it be fun and exciting?

It should be noted that the questions and concerns other researchers bring to their quest for methodology and methods will necessarily lead to assessing the methods given here differently. We make no firm endorsement of one analysis method over another. Instead, we recommend that researchers use their search as an opportunity to let the principles of Organic Inquiry speak to them in liminal consciousness, and to apply whatever personal subjectivities might be used in the research project to the evaluation of which methods and procedures to incorporate.

Because the interview of participants is at the heart of an Organic Inquiry as a data collection method, we begin with a review of interview analysis.

Kvale's Interview Analysis

Kvale (1996) points out that analysis in the interview method is woven throughout the research project, rather than being a discrete procedure applied at a particular point. "A recognition of the pervasiveness of interpretation throughout an entire interview inquiry may counteract a common overemphasis on methods of analysis as *the* one way to find the meaning of interviews" (p. 205, italics original). When a researcher asks the interviewee to clarify or further explain some aspect of the interview, this is an early form of analysis because the researcher has implicitly or explicitly assessed that the statement as first made might be expanded to provide greater or more significant detail. "The analysis may also, to varying degrees, be built into the interview situation itself...the researcher may attempt to confirm or reject his or her hypothesis during the interview" p. 178).

As researcher and interviewee work together to achieve a fully told story about the experience or phenomenon under investigation, they are also participating in a form of analysis of understanding. "The qualitative research interview is particularly well suited for employing leading questions to check repeatedly the reliability of the interviewees' answers, as well as to verify the interviewer's interpretations" (p. 158).

The transcription process is another form of analysis, particularly if not verbatim, but rather allowing the transcriptionist to apply some editorial framework for transferring speech to text, such as cleaning up grammar, deleting ums, uhs, and other such non-lexicals, or reorganizing rapid exchange dialogue when researcher and interviewee interrupt and complete each other's sentences. "Every transcription from one context to another involves a series of judgments and decisions" (p. 163). Translating speech to text gets even more complicated when simple expressive factors are considered, such as:

Where does a sentence end? Where is there a pause? How long is a silence before it becomes a pause in a conversation? Does a specific pause belong to the subject or to the interviewer? And if the emotional aspects of the conversation are included, for instance "tense voice," "giggling," "nervous laughter," and so on, the intersubjective reliability of the transcription could develop into a research project of its own. (p. 164)

Following this caution, it is clear that even the transformation of verbatim transcript to vignette that adds no words or interpretations to the interviewee's original story, but merely eliminates redundancy and shortens the story to highlight a particular incident or viewpoint, is a form of judgment-making analysis.

After making these points that analysis occurs all the way along in a research project, Kvale mentions five specific methods that could be applied to interviews to produce more generative knowledge, which can be simply identified as condensing, categorizing, structuring, interpreting, and free form.

In condensing—which is the general approach taken by Giorgi's (1975) descriptive phenomenological method—"long statements are compressed into briefer statements in which the main sense of what is said is rephrased in a few words" (Kvale, p. 192).

In categorizing, large amounts of text are reduced and structured according to some schema such as presence/absence. The six principles of Organic Inquiry could be used as such a schema. "The categories can be developed in advance or they can arise ad hoc during the analysis; they may be taken from theory or from the vernacular, as well as from the interviewees' own idioms" (p. 192). For example, in our study, we were careful to wait until the data "spoke to us" and told us what the category should be called before assigning a label.

Narrative structuring focuses on the way the information is told, creating of disparate details a coherent meaning-making story. "Structuring through narratives will usually reduce the interview text; it may however, also expand it by developing the potentialities of meaning in a simple interview story into more elaborate narratives" (p. 193).

In interpreting, the decontextualized interview that is represented by the transcript or vignette is recontextualized within a larger frame of reference. "The context for interpretation of a statement may, for example, be provided by the entire interview or by a theory" (p. 193).

Finally, in the free form, or ad hoc analysis approach, "a variety of commonsense approaches to the interview text, as well as sophisticated textual or quantitative methods, can be used to bring out the meanings of different parts of the material" (p. 193).

To evaluate an approach taken from Kvale's suggestions for interview analysis, I (Deah) tried the interpretive approach, even though detailed steps are not given in his book. Without other introduction to the hermeneutic method, I relied on explanations embedded in Kvale's various chapters to elicit the following procedure for interpretive analysis of interviews. The procedure is presented as a series of steps, because that made it easy for me follow as I developed and performed the process.

1. Read a participant's transcript until a sense emerges of the gestalt of her/his individual experience.

2. Write a summary statement of that gestalt for the transcript.

3. Apply several meaning seeking questions to the text (transcript) and to the recollection of the interview:

    a) How has [the topic of investigation] operated in this person's experience?
    b) What kind of transformation did this person experience?
    c) How did this experience change how this person interacted with her/his world?
    d) What opened up in this person's psyche because of this experience?

4. With each question in turn in mind, reread the transcript and note what the text has to say about these several questions.

5. Rewrite the summary statement to reflect the various questions above.

6. Repeat these steps with each transcript.

7. Write a statement that tells the story of [the topic of investigation] and transformation as told through the combined voices of participants and researcher(s).

8. Apply to the combined story the questions previously used in interrogating the individual texts.

9. Write a statement that gives the derived meaning of the experience of [the topic of investigation] and transformation in the population studied.

I (Deah) found using this interpretive analysis method to be very time consuming, although that could have been due in part to ferreting out an unfamiliar procedure from various chapters of Kvale's book. For the purposes of subsequent research projects, I was not confident that the steps above represent a true hermeneutic circle, nor was I confident that the final interpretation I achieved had the level of significance I would have wanted for a dissertation project.

While it is possible that significance would be apparent with a larger number of participants' stories to review, it is unclear whether this method would answer all general research questions that novice researchers might pose. Nor is it clear that the interpretive method would provide the sort of rich description an Organic Inquiry is after, since unique detail is abstracted at each level of the process. We might expect that participants who are untrained in research would have a difficult time following the steps and producing varying levels of summary statements.

While this analysis method is not strikingly inconsistent with the tenets of Organic Inquiry, it did not resonate enough with mind, body, or Spirit to become the analysis method we selected for our projects.

Kvale reminded the researcher that analysis occurs as much in unplanned interactions and choices during interviews and transcription, even in design and recruitment, as it does at a specific point in the research project. He identifies five analysis methods that might be particularly well suited to interview studies. Kvale's book is highly recommended to novice researchers who are attempting an interview method for the first time.

Riessman's Narrative Analysis

Because Organic Inquiry puts such a premium on the storied nature of ideographic knowing, we evaluated narrative analysis. Riessman (1993) noted that narrative analysis is essentially about finding the structure of stories; that is, how stories are told. The story itself is the focus of the investigation, rather than a particular phenomenon around which the story is told. Through explicating the structure, the meaning of personal experience can be known. An important point to remember for interviewing is that "in telling about an experience, [the speaker is] also creating a self— how [she or he] wants to be known....(p. 11).

Riessman points to additional issues regarding transcribing interview tapes:

> Should they include silences, false starts, emphases, nonlexicals like "uhms," discourse markers like "y'know" or "so," overlapping speech, and other signs of listener participation in the narrative? Should they give clauses separate lines and display rhythmic and poetic structures by grouping lines? Not simply technical questions, these seemingly mundane choices of what to include and how to arrange and display the text have serious implications for how a reader will understand the narrative. (p. 12)

Riessman gave several models for analyzing narratives, of which Labov's (1972, 1982) is held to be the most widely used or adapted. Labov looks for six elements: "an abstract...orientation...sequence of events...(significance and meaning of the action, attitude of the narrator), resolution...and code (returns the perspective to the present)" (Riessman, pp. 18-19). In contrast, Gee's (1986) model focuses on the oral and tonal features of storytelling such as "changes in pitch, pauses, and other features that punctuate speech..." (p. 19).

In describing the limitations of narrative analysis, Riessman stated that narrative methods "require attention to subtlety: nuances of speech, organization of a response, local contexts of production, social discourses that shape what is said, and what cannot be spoken" (p. 69). The narrative methods would be appropriate for investigating the structure of how research participants interact with an experience, or how they construct meaningfulness from their experience, or how discussion of such experience changes something in how they interact.

Although a narrative method of analysis may be able to be used for an Organic Inquiry—especially one that focuses directly on the act of storytelling—it would not seem to meet the requirements of answering a broad general range of research questions, be easy for participants to do, or producing specific in-depth description of phenomena of investigation. In short, it did not resonate for us with heart, body, or soul.

Several Options Suggested by Miles and Huberman

Miles and Huberman (1994) define analysis as "consisting of three concurrent flows of activity: data reduction, data display, and conclusion drawing/verification" (p. 10). Regarding data reduction, they prefer to develop a coding schema before data collection, and then use the schema to help identify pertinent information embedded in the data.

> "...we prefer [creating] a provisional 'start list' of codes prior to fieldwork. That list comes from the conceptual framework, list of research questions, hypotheses, problem areas, and/or key variables that the researcher brings to the study" (p. 58).

Alternatively, a grounded theory type of approach would proceed more inductively:

Initial data are collected, written up, and reviewed line by line, typically within a paragraph. Beside or below the paragraph, categories or labels are generated, and a list of them grows. The labels are reviewed and, typically, a slightly more abstract category is attributed to several incidents or observations....another idea: Read field notes for regularly occurring phrases, and with an eye to surprising or counterintuitive material that needs to be clarified elsewhere in the notes or in the field. (p. 58)

So that neither deductive nor inductive approaches overlook salient features of participant stories that do not fit the preconceived "start list," Miles and Huberman point out that any set of codes should change and evolve as the research progresses.

Among their many suggestions for analytic procedures is a sequential analysis drawn from Chesler (1987, in Miles & Huberman, p. 87). Appearing to be elegantly simple in its instruction—although actual use may be more complicated than one expects—and to lead to some measure of clarity in the results it can produce, the Chesler steps in brief are:

1. Underline key terms

2. Restate key phrases

3. Reduce phrases, create clusters

4. Reduce clusters, attach labels

5. Generalize about clusters

6. Generate mini-theory

7. Integrate theory into explanatory framework.

Although not specified in Chesler's instruction, it seemed natural to perform step 3 by way of a matrix display (wherein horizontal and vertical axes make cross referencing easy) which would then be revised in step 4. This procedure is particularly well suited for use in grounded theory studies, and might be appropriate for describing and developing generative knowledge about the elusive phenomenon of the sort studied in Organic Inquiries.

Other display types presented in Miles and Huberman (1994) such as the Content-Analytic Summary Table (p. 183), the Causal Flowchart (p. 225), Overlapping Clusters (p. 249), the network or hierarchical tree diagram (p. 133), and the Cognitive Map (p. 135), could be used to display data analyzed with the Chesler steps.

For variety, the Folk Taxonomy (p. 133) might be a procedure that participants could easily use—perhaps even during the interview session—that would provide the researcher with further insight into how participants make meaning of their unique experience. The Transcript as Poem (p. 110) is an idea that appeals on the basis of being a data reduction display that adds to, rather than takes away from, the impact of participants' stories. As an example, Belanger (1998) wrote haiku based on her participants' interviews that brought her topic into sharp and creative focus.

On the whole, Chesler's procedure for sequential analysis appears to meet several of the evaluation criteria we hold for an Organic Inquiry: it is likely to answer the research question, it would probably ensure the generation of rich description, and may be satisfying in terms of the researcher's natural cognitive style. However, it may be too complex or tedious for research participants to follow without training.

Nothing in the procedure rubs against the tenets of Organic Inquiry, and liminal information could be processed alongside data generated from other sources. Even so, it might be said that sequential analysis lacks an embodied resonance (but this will differ for different researchers), although it provides some measure (or illusion!) of cognitive confidence.

Moustakas's Guidelines for Heuristic Inquiry

The heuristic method is several steps closer to the tone of Organic Inquiry than the data analysis approaches reviewed so far in that "the self of the researcher is present throughout the process and, while understanding the phenomenon with increasing depth, the researcher also experiences growing self-awareness and self-knowledge. Heuristic processes incorporate creative self-processes and self-discoveries" (Moustakas, 1990, p. 9).

The heuristic approach has grown out of a foundation that resonates with the transpersonal grounding of Organic Inquiry: Maslow's work on self-actualizing persons, Juror's studies on self-disclosure, Polaner's explorations of tacit knowing, Buber's I-thou valuing in the dialogic relationship, among others (pp. 9-10).

Still, some essential distinctions exist between Organic and heuristic approaches to research. Organic Inquiry places a premium on participant and researcher storytelling (Jennifer Clements, et. al., 1998, p.125); heuristic inquiry searches "for qualities, conditions, and relationships that underlie a fundamental question, issue, or concern" (Moustakas, 1990, p. 11). Organic Inquiry directs the researcher to "travel to the liminal realm, gather experience, and return to intellectually integrate it" (Jennifer Clements, 2000, p. 1); heuristic inquiry simply allows the possibility that the researcher may become "entranced by visions, images, and dreams that connect" (Moustakas, p. 11). Organic Inquiry emphasizes processes in partnership with Spirit (Clements, 2001); heuristic inquiry "requires a return to the self, a recognition of self-awareness, and a valuing of one's own experience" (Moustakas, p. 13).

Analysis in Jennifer Clements' (2001) revised version of Organic Inquiry holds participants' stories up to the Jungian typology of feeling, intuition, sensation, and thinking in order to elicit four types of meaning.

> During these feeling, intuitive, thinking, and sensate examinations of the data, the researcher will not only be searching for understanding, but will also be recording her or his own individual responses which will be part of the description of transformative change in the third part of the analysis. (Jennifer Clements, 2001, p. 176).

Analysis in a heuristic inquiry imposes no organizing schema and is free form in its instructions that involve immersion, or indwelling, in the data; taking a break then reviewing all again; making notes, and identifying themes and qualities from which is constructed a depiction of the experience under investigation; checking the depiction against the original data for "fit"; adjusting the depiction if necessary; and repeating the process with other data sets (such as interview transcripts and notes).

Then taking the individual depictions together, the researcher is called on to develop the universal qualities and themes from which are formed a group or composite depiction of the experience. Once more, the researcher returns to the original data to select exemplars, editing individual data into profiles that illustrate the core themes. Finally, a creative synthesis is made that:

> tes a recognition of tacit-intuitive awarenesses of the research, the knowledge that has been incubating over months through processes of immersion, illumination, and explication of the phenomenon investigated. The researcher as scientist-artist develops an aesthetic rendition of the themes and essential meanings...taps into imaginative and contemplative sources of knowledge and insight in synthesizing the experience, in presenting the discovery of essences... (p. 52)

Just how the qualities and themes are to be explicated, or how the universal core essences are to be developed is left unstated in Moustakas's (1990) outline guide of procedures. On this score, a novice researcher is no better off following the heuristic process than attempting an Organic Inquiry. In a project that used a process similar to the heuristic procedure we discovered that we needed to import steps similar to Chesler's sequential analysis in order to find qualities, themes, and core essences. Whether a researcher uses Organic Inquiry or heuristic inquiry, some manner of systematic examination of the data will be needed. Neither approach is clear about exactly how to proceed when reaching that stage of the research.

The heuristic inquiry approach resonates in part with the tenets of Organic Inquiry, may be likely to answer similar research questions, and provide rich description of the phenomenon under investigation with the help of sequential analysis. It is unknown how difficult the procedures would be for participants to follow, and a possible danger would be that participants would jump to the sequential analysis steps in order to produce a product, at the sacrifice of indwelling, writing depictions, and note making—important parts of the heuristic process.

Anderson's Intuitive Inquiry and Resonance Panels

Like the Organic methodology, intuitive inquiry is positioned as a transpersonal approach to research. Rather than a central concern for partnering with Spirit for transformative change, intuitive inquiry "places attributes such as intuition, compassion, immediate apprehension of meaning, and service to society's disenfranchised persons as central to scientific or empirical inquiry in psychology" (Anderson, 1998, p. 70). As a specific approach to research, its procedures can be used alone, or combined with other approaches, such as Organic Inquiry.

A particularly unique feature of intuitive inquiry is its emphasis on sympathetic resonance as a validation procedure for direct apprehension of knowing. "Through the validation procedures of consonant, dissonant, and neutral sympathetic resonance, subgroup by subgroup, a type of mapping of the validity of a research finding could be done" (pp. 74-75).

Intuitive inquiry builds on some tenets of heuristic inquiry, as does the Organic approach, especially in terms of the researcher being an instrument of knowing. "The depth of the researcher's intuitive understanding gives a universal voice and character to the research findings....enlivening the research with...richness of inquiry and expression..." (pp. 75-76). Similar to Organic Inquiry, but without conceptualizing these factors as gifts of Spirit or travels to the liminal realm, the intuitive approach:

> advocates expanded states of intuitive awareness, including...various altered states of consciousness, active dreaming and dream incubation, mystical vision and audition, intentional imaging, kinesthetic and somatic awareness, and states of consciousness more typically associated with the artistic process than with science...(p. 76).

Concerned with issues of validity, Anderson (2000) cautions that "like observational data, intuitions oblige corroborative evidence since they are subject to error and bias" (p. 32). She presents a model for analysis that flows back and forth between the subjective and the objective in a kind of hermeneutic circle, or "cycles of interpretation" (p. 32), that is similar in process to the interpretive analysis evaluated above, although different in terms of making explicit the researcher's personal context.

> At the outset of the research endeavor, the intuitive researcher initially identifies her or his values and assumptions through active and connected engagement with the experience studied and then uses these values and assumptions as hermeneutical lenses to explore and analyze similar experiences in others. (p. 32).

Introspection, reflection, documentation, repeated data review, and generalizing to themes—while being aware of various lenses of intuitive perception such as visual, auditory, proprioceptive, blends, context, etc—become the template for an intuitive analysis process. An embodied or cognitive-somatic resonance is used as the meter for gauging when the cycles of interpretation are complete, when the essential themes are found, and distinguishing what is essential from that which is significant but tangential. It might be said that the first level of analysis is also additional data gathering by the researcher of that which is presented to her or his various intuitive senses.

At some point, the researcher notes "consistent patterns and clusters of ideas in her or his understanding of the topic" (pp. 36-37). This is an important difference from sequential analysis which notes patterns and clusters embedded in the data itself. Also, where Anderson (2000) uses the term *lenses,* Chesler (1987) might use the term *phrases;* where Anderson uses the term *clusters,* Chesler would appear to use the term *labels*—an inconsistency in languaging that is confusing for novice researchers attempting to understand various methods.

Capping an intuitive inquiry is what Anderson (2000) calls a *resonance panel* (p. 37)—a form of cooperative inquiry group (Heron, 1996) that reviews themes distilled to that point, and with their own embodied intuitive resonance, modifies, refines, and synthesizes the themes, moving the research findings towards deeper validity and generalizable statements. This differs from Organic Inquiry's quest for transformative change which is more about results of experiential or research processes rather than the products of analyzed data.

Intuitive inquiry is quite compatible with Organic Inquiry, even though participant stories may be augmented by literature texts as original data, and hermeneutic analysis would lead the researcher deeper into interpretation than the Organic approach intends. From the Organic Inquiry point of view, intuitive inquiry seeks to arrive at knowledge claims that can be handed over to readers as completed projects. In contrast, a central principle of Organic Inquiry is to present a model for knowing and knowledge seeking that readers can join, albeit at a distance, in order to arrive at their own understanding instead of the understanding that is pre-processed by the researcher.

Intuitive inquiry seems a sophisticated approach to analysis that would be challenging for research participants' engagement, and difficult if not intimidating for general readers. While it could produce rich description of experiences under investigation, it seems more likely to answer other types of questions than those designed to primarily seek out description. Rather than elucidating the characteristics of a phenomenon itself, intuitive inquiry may be better suited to answer: how is the experience under investigation meaningful to the study population?

We hope that this chapter has provided a comparative look at several possible choices for augmenting the data analysis methods in an Organic Inquiry. These are not the only options, of course, and we encourage novice and seasoned researchers alike to carefully review a range of possibilities before settling on those that will be most appropriate for each individual study.

Possible Data Analysis Methods For My Study:

CHAPTER 7

The How

Designing an Organic Inquiry

An explicit set of procedures for an Organic Inquiry is lacking in the original source material for this methodology. Each researcher is called on to take this as a challenge to be "in partnership with Spirit" (Clements, 2001, p. 38) from the outset of the design phase of research, and to apply the Jungian typology of sensing, feeling, intuiting, and thinking as a meta-structure for the design (p. 168). That is, researchers are expected to use analysis procedures that go beyond the linear and rational thought process by also holding data up to bodily senses, emotions of the heart, and intuitive resonances.

For my (Deah's) project, the idea of partnering with Spirit meant that while I critically chose the options for the various elements of the research design, I also evaluated those options with the extra-analytic faculties of somatic resonance, emotional appeal, and intuitive or direct knowing.

To assist the design process, it may be helpful to hold in mind five criteria that all procedures and the overall design can follow:

1. The overall design and individual procedures resonate with the tone and tenets of Organic Inquiry, especially in regard to the principles that research can be conducted as if it were sacred, and can lead to transformative learning.

2. All features of the study help answer the guiding question or hypothesis.

3. Procedures generate rich and meaningful description that can lead to nomothetic findings without giving overwhelming tangential detail.

4. Some kind of group inquiry or group response opportunity is incorporated into the design that resonates with the research question, analyzes data, and generates data synthesis.

5. Procedures are satisfying to follow; that is, they resonate with the researcher's own style of working, fit with an Organic Inquiry's intentions for using some form of a Jungian typology for data gathering and data analysis, and are fun to do.

Research begins not with data collection, but with the myriad of process and value decisions an investigator makes in articulating the research question, and in selecting methodology, method, procedures, and participants. The criteria above could be applied to qualitative methodologies other than Organic Inquiries. They should be viewed as background requirements against which to shape the context in which the research designer makes more specific design decisions.

When using an innovative research methodology, it can be helpful to supervising committees to understand how each feature of the methodology correlates to one's research design. It is useful to be explicit regarding how each element and procedure fulfills a specific function in relation to the unique features of the Organic methodology.

Recruiting Participants In Partnership with Spirit

For some researchers, getting all the participants needed for one's study can be the most difficult aspect of any project. Getting just the right participants who will contribute immeasurably to one's study can be even more difficult.

Research supervisors will have much good advice on recruiting participants, and since each study will have its own idiosyncratic needs, addressing the many possibilities for recruitment is beyond the scope of this primer. However, we do point out that the recruitment phase of a project is a particularly appropriate time to remember that in an Organic Inquiry, one is in partnership with Spirit.

In our study, for example, we recruited in three primary ways: by posting fliers, by letters that asked others to send us interview candidates, and by directly asking appropriate individuals. In all three recruitment strategies, in order to develop lists of potential posting places, letter recipients, and direct recruitment individuals, I (Deah) first went into the liminal domain to allow options that my logical mind had not considered, and to confirm or disconfirm what my logical mind had decided. In this way I allowed myself to partner with the interconnecting aspect of Spirit that flowed through liminal domain. After that Steve and I discussed what we thought were the best options to pursue.

As interview candidates begin calling in response to recruitment strategies, researchers can again be in partnership with Spirit in order to discern when borderline candidates should be accepted into the study. This is a particularly important use of being in partnership with Spirit when the study is not filling up as quickly as the researchers would like. It is also one of the times when having the support of a research associate is very helpful.

Data Gathering in Conscious and Liminal Domains

Much has already been said in this primer about data gathering in an Organic Inquiry, and volumes have been written by others about the art of interviewing—one of the main data gathering methods in this approach. This section focuses on the dual nature of data gathering in an Organic study; that is, gathering data in the conscious and the liminal domains.

The in-depth interview method is at the heart of Organic inquiries. Whether unstructured or semi-structured, the Organic researcher aims to allow participants' stories to unfold in a natural way (Kvale, 1996; Rubin & Rubin, 1995). The interview is conversational, and mutually disclosing such that the artificial barriers between investigator and participant dissolve into two co-researchers looking together at the experience of interest.

The interview may also prompt critical reflection and examination of assumptions, which is similar to processes of discourse analysis and transformative learning (Mezirow, 1997, 1998). As such, the interview method satisfies the Organic elements of the personal (relating personal story), and the relational (mutually empathic disclosure, and commonality-finding through natural and reflective conversation), while allowing the potential for the transformative (should interviewee or researcher achieve some spontaneous insight into the nature of the experience under investigation) (Elias, 1997).

Novice interviewers may find it helpful to prepare an interview guide. This list of questions keeps an in-depth interview on track, and helps manage time in the session—two crucial elements of a successful interview. In a casual atmosphere, some interviewees will naturally talk about many things that are only indirectly related to the formal research question. An interview guide helps rein in these wanderings. It also helps the researcher to remember to ask the important questions. Depending on how the researcher plans to analyze the data, having a few standardized questions to ask of all interviewees can make analysis work much easier later on, and moves the findings closer into the realm of generative knowledge.

Another primary data gathering method used in Organic studies to date has been the cooperative inquiry process (Heron, 1996). Here, participants work as a group to elicit data, each sparking new directions in thinking for others.

In an inquiry group, the potential exists to gain pieces of individual stories that might not be offered during one-on-one interviews, simply because more than one person is listening and responding to each participant's story. This group dynamic factor thus can potentially increase the depth and breadth of the data that is gathered in an Organic Inquiry.

On the other hand, group dynamics can make for very tricky situations for researchers, who risk losing data if they are not experienced at group facilitation. Researchers who make a cooperative inquiry process the primary data gathering method of their Organic study will want to be certain they can handle the participants who monopolize conversations as well as those find it more difficult to disclose and discuss personal information in groups of strangers.

In addition to expertly handling these group dynamics challenges, researchers will also need to have a flexible group agenda, and to keep a sharp eye on time-keeping in order that all research protocols that must be completed during group sessions are afforded enough time.

Although time and funding may mediate against it, cooperative inquiry groups can be especially rewarding when conducted in the context of a several day retreat. Such a format would allow both group inquiry and individual interviews, as well as social time, and activities that invite all participants into partnership with Spirit.

In the Liminal Domain

In Chapter 2 we provided one simple process for traveling to the liminal domain and gathering information there. This is the heart of the three-step process model of Organic Inquiry—and the third step is to integrate the information into the rest of the data gathered and analyzed. Now we look at other ways that researchers and participants can access information in the liminal domain.

In a psychological sense, the liminal domain can be understood as the subconscious mind, and its language is that of visual symbols and other meta-verbal communication such as emotional responses and bodily sensations. It can be accessed by means other than the kind of guided visualization or meditative journey we outlined in Chapter 2.

Dreams might be considered products of the liminal domain. Even when the topic of investigation is something other than dreams, researchers might receive important information about the design, or analysis, or other procedures as a result of paying attention to their dreams. As part of the researcher's journal it could be fruitful to keep a dream journal in which recurring symbols and themes are noted and related to how the research is developing.

Stream of consciousness journaling might be a way for researchers to allow information from the liminal domain to break through into consciousness. The process is simple and could be accomplished in a number of ways. One way might be to spend 20 minutes at the end of each interview session, or at the end of each day during the research period just writing the impressions that come to mind. If this seems too purpose-free, try recording what you observed about the interviewee, or what you noticed about yourself. Do not use this time to problem solve. Imagine, if it helps, that you are giving Spirit a chance to speak to you through the journaling.

Making art products—whether painting, clay, line drawing, jewelry, mixed media collage, or other crafts—is a wonderful, non-verbal way to be in the flow of the partnership with Spirit. In addition to researchers using this method of connecting with the liminal domain for their own purposes during the research period, incorporating an expressive arts activity into the research design can serve to bring participants into the liminal domain as well.

Projective expression is a fancy term for allowing the subconscious mind to connect with meaningful symbols without being in a dream state. In the realm of psychological assessment, tests such as the Rorschach and the Thematic Apperception Test are expressions of projective imagery. In the realm of the esoteric arts, tarot cards, runes, the I-Ching and other forms of augury or divination are expressions of projective imagery. In an Organic Inquiry, projective expression might be used as a way to connect with the liminal realm and gather information through what one sees in the item being observed.

Various modes of dance and music could serve to stimulate the researchers' and participants' travel to the liminal realm. Or, for those who are creative in this direction, dance or music could be created in the liminal domain and used as the products of information one brings back to integrate with other data.

In this short review it is clear that researchers have a range of ways available to them for journeying to the liminal domain and accessing or gathering information there as part of their Organic Inquiry. Anything that shifts one out of the normal consciousness of the logical mind can be a means for journeying into the liminal realm.

Data Analysis within an Organic Inquiry

Chapter 6 reviewed several data analysis methods that might be compatible with the intentions of Organic Inquiry. This section addresses the reality of using a methodology that encourages rich description—-the fact that the researchers will soon become inundated by overwhelming volumes of raw data.

Managing Mountains of Data

One of the most important things to know before embarking on an Organic Inquiry is that it will likely generate mountains of data, no matter which analysis method is used. A carefully organized data management scheme is essential, whether data is primarily kept in computer files, subdirectories, hard drives, and back-up disks, or printed out and sorted into boxes, drawers, all available flat surfaces within an arm's reach of the desk, and strategically located piles on the floor.

Exactly how one organizes the data for easy retrieval depends in part on the nature of the inquiry, and the flow of the research design. For example, Deah tends to keep as much as possible on the computer, and what hard copies she generated for her dissertation project fit into half a file drawer. Those included:

- hand notes taken during phone screening of potential participants

- signed consent forms and blank extras

- reviewed/revised vignettes if not returned by email attachment

- hard copy questionnaires completed at the interview and blank extras

- hand notes taken during interviews and other procedures

- photos taken of creative expression products, and their negatives

- any supplemental materials used during interviews and group session

- interview and group session audio tapes

- hand written reflexive journal notes

Steve, who was Deah's co-researcher on the dissertation project, tends to print out everything in order to work by hand. This kind of dual system provides extra security in case of a computer crash before work has been put on disks. He also finds it easier to read from printouts than a computer screen and this method allowed him to work in his living room, on the couch or more comfortable chairs than the computer area. He managed all this paper by carefully organizing items by type and stacking or filing them in chronological order, or whatever other system seemed appropriate at the time. He ended up with a full "bank box" file by the end. He was able to secure it's safety by simply placing items where they would not be available to persons visiting his home.

On the computer—as just one of many organizational schemas—each interviewee could have a subdirectory, and all material pertaining to that person can be located in separate files under that subdirectory. Included as separate files in each person's subdirectory would be:

- clean copy of verbatim interview transcript

- vignette develop from transcripts as sent to interviewee

- vignettes as revised by interviewee

- interviewee's self-analysis

- transcript with first level analysis markings

As data is pulled out of the transcripts and set into new documents, a data analysis subdirectory could be created. In this subdirectory all interviewees could have further subdirectories so that locating analysis on an individual person can be fast and easy. Under each person's subdirectory might be located different documents on each step of the analysis process. In that way, mistakes in analysis and confusion in findings are easy to trace. For example, in Deah's dissertation project her data analysis subdirectory resembled this order for each interviewee:

C:\\Dissertation Project\Data analysis
    \Interviewee 1
        \Phase 1 analysis
            \Interviewee 1 own analysis
            \Unsorted
            \Sorted
            \Pruned
        \Phase 2 analysis
            \Combined (with co-researcher's pruned
                analysis)

When all analysis steps had been completed on each interviewees' transcript, and when Deah's work and Steve's work on each interviewee had been combined, a further organization was needed to manage the next steps. A new subdirectory was created where the pruned data from each interviewee was combined into one pruned master data document. Then further analysis work was done from this combined master document:

C:\\Dissertation Project\Data analysis
    \Interviewee 1
    \Interviewee 2 (etc)
    \Phase 3
        \Combined master
        \Further pruning
        \Phase 3 sorting
        \Synthesis

The key to managing large volumes of data in an Organic Inquiry is to have a data organization schema that makes it simple to work with your data at each step of the process, and that makes it fast and stress-free to retrace your steps, or to find the results of prior steps, when necessary. Using your research design as a guide in constructing your organization schema can be helpful, and might ensure that no part of the design—as approved in your proposal—is inadvertently skipped or forgotten in the excitement of the project as it unfolds.

Interpreting Findings

Interpreting the findings of any qualitative research study is perhaps the most difficult part of the project. Interpreting findings in an Organic Inquiry is no exception. Data analysis gives us the generative patterns, but how do we decide what they really mean? While we are not experts at research interpretation, we can offer how we approached this daunting task in our three Organic studies. Other researchers will no doubt develop their own approaches.

I (Steve) did my interpretations by first allowing my conscious mind to recede and moving my consciousness into a liminal state through breath, and perhaps movement if I found it necessary. From this heightened vantage point various words and phrases that resonated with the research question would appear to me as though they were highlighted on the page. I could then gather them into groupings that seemed to fit together.

At certain points I had intuitive knowings of the labels for different sets of data. These came to me from the data itself while I was in this liminal realm. After I had completed assessing the data in this manner, I could allow my rational mind to again come into play and concretely discern what meanings might be associated with the various data sets.

While Steve started from the perspective of the liminal domain, after my groupings of data had names themselves, I (Deah) tended to come into interpretation from the opposite direction. I reviewed the patterns that had surfaced from the data, and the categories that the data had sorted themselves into. I asked myself: What can be said about these findings? What do I know now that I did not know before I talked with the first interviewee?

Then I took each category in turn and began writing in answer to these questions. Sometimes, the writing took on a life or its own, and I had to return to the data to make sure what I was saying was really supported in the data. When this iteration of interpretation came to a stopping point, I did with the interpretation process what I had done with the transcripts; that is, I took the categories and the research question to the altar of the study's partnership with Spirit. Then, in much the same way as Steve had done, I entered the liminal domain and waited for deeper meanings and understanding to come to me.

Connecting the findings and my interpretations with the pertinent literature also provided another opportunity to see meanings in the results our data had created. Our findings not only yielded some generative knowledge about our research questions, it also served to confirm elements of others' studies and hypotheses. Looking for how one's findings connects with other researchers' work, then, adds another dimension to the art of data interpretation.

The primary point we want to make about interpretation is that in an Organic Inquiry, traveling into the liminal domain should not be reserved simply for data gathering, or for being in touch with Spirit. The liminal domain can help with a variety of research tasks, and is a valuable resource in interpreting findings.

Notes on Chapter 7

How I'll recruit participants:

Thoughts on how I'll organize my data:

Types of data gathering and analysis methods I could use:

Other thoughts about how I'll organize my project:

CHAPTER 8

🌿

Addressing Specific Questions
About Organic Inquiry

In this chapter we address some of the obvious questions that novice researcher, and others, may have about Organic Inquiry that have not been fully discussed in previous chapters.

Can anyone do this type of research, or does one have to be a "believer" in a specific form of Spirituality to use it?

Organic Inquiry as a methodology for human sciences research lays no claim to any one religious or Spiritual tradition. Nothing in the principles or the process models of this approach to disciplined knowing dictates any specific Spiritual practice in favor of another. In fact, Jennifer Clements, et. al. appear to have intentionally left vague their definition of the sacred so that anyone might find the reflection of their own Spirituality in this methodology. We think that any concept of the sacred and any Spiritual practice can be incorporated into an Organic Inquiry. For a "non-believer," using this methodology can be an opportunity to study oneself and one's relation to possibilities of the sacred, and to experiment with Spiritual practices as a study within a study.

Can researchers substitute some other type of thinking for the Spiritual aspects, such as a purely scientific mind-set, and still do this work effectively?

In our opinion, one of the things that makes the Organic approach unique and powerful is its emphasis on viewing research as a sacred endeavor, and pursuing knowing in partnership with Spirit.

Rather than degrading research by incorporating these aspects, we think the analytic mode of knowing is enhanced by being expanded in this way.

Other aspects of an Organic Inquiry that are unique and powerful are that of traveling to the liminal realm to gather data, and to possibly be inspired or instructed by the tests and challenges of the chthonic, and the guides and teachers of the numinous. These are integral features of this approach to research that make explicit the role of the unconscious—and other sources of knowing and creativity—in ways that other research methods tend to leave unacknowledged. We believe that researchers who are uncomfortable with incorporating these important features into their research might find a different methodology more to their liking.

What are some possible parameters of definitions of the sacred that might allow broader use? Or is this even a good idea? Would it disrupt the methodology to try to do so?

Concepts of the sacred can be as broad, or as narrow, as one desires. It could be said that everything is inherently sacred, or it could be said that nothing is inherently sacred, or any position between the two. For some the concept is reserved for certain special places, persons, objects, times, etc. For others the concept can include all things that exist. The idea of the sacred is very subjective and contextual, all depending on who is making the judgment of when something is or is not, or about what may or may not be, sacred. For us it is a state of conscious mind-body-Spirit-environment relationship – the web of life. In practice, one chooses whatever definition of the sacred that suits one's purpose, and these definitions may be subject to change as one has more experiences of the sacred, however it might be defined.

Broadening the definition to allow those who do not believe in concepts of the sacred has both advantages and disadvantages. On the one hand it allows those with a more positivist empirical mindset to use the methodology and perhaps be transformed such that they are then able to recognize the sacred. This may come as a welcome, or possibly unwelcome, surprise, depending on the person's desire to allow for open, unfettered growth and the breaking up of old ways of seeing things. This is common with scientists, who wish primarily to learn and understand our universe.

However, Organic Inquiry could as easily be used as a way for those who wish to disprove the concept of sacredness. And they might well succeed, for to attempt to use the methodology with such disregard for being in partnership with Spirit would likely subconsciously or even consciously block their ability to move into the liminal domain or even to relax their minds. Thus such researchers might garner what they would consider "proof" that the sacred does not exist.

We believe both of these things might inevitably happen and over time these experiments will significantly strengthen Organic Inquiry, rather than disrupt it. So we simply accept it and look forward to what others' experiences will bring.

How important is enjoying oneself to truly embodying the methodology?

Different researchers are likely to have different opinions about this question. We think that when any undertaking is enjoyable that that is a sign that one is in natural partnership with Spirit. Being aware that Spirit is flowing in and through oneself has sometimes been described as having a sense of radical aliveness (Curry, 2003; Moss, 1986).

Embodying a research methodology may seem like a strange concept. Most research is very heady, or cognitively oriented, in its approach to discovering information, and it has no desire to embody its tenets, nor does it have a place for things like a concept of the sacred.

On the other hand, we see in Organic Inquiry a high priority on recognizing the sacred and embodying one's approach to research, because it places a priority on personal, subjective knowledge. Learning to experience life through the body is an entirely different approach to experience and meaning, and allows one to learn things that are simply not accessible to those who believe their minds are the sole arbiters of experience.

As we proposed in the last chapter, recognizing the sacred can be as simple as recognizing the web of relationships in which we all live our lives. We look at this is a very concrete physical way, so in our view embodying the methodology is already something we all do everyday in all the things we do. We realize this awareness may not be true for everyone and it may take special effort to bring the research into one's body. It takes some practice to feel things in one's body and we are not taught to do so. In fact we are often discouraged from it. But because of the kind of information our bodies have to offer us, and the meanings made available by this methodology, we feel it is absolutely necessary to embody the methodology in order to successfully follow the steps of the Organic approach. We must feel it to do it.

How important is it to "live" the methodology in your life while using it as an approach to research?

In our view, one cannot help but live the Organic methodology, and for it to live the researchers, during a research project. "Living the methodology" might be understood as becoming aware of how the principles of the sacred, the personal, the relational, the chthonic, the numinous, and the transformative are already alive and moving through one's life and work, and how one already, naturally, journeys to the liminal domain, gathers information, and returns to integrate it into their understanding of themselves, and the world they are a part of.

What is meant by subjectivity as a tool of knowing?

Knowing can be achieved not only by the mind through analysis and reasoning, it can also be gained through intuition, somatic sensation, emotion, and the elusive function we might call *felt meaningfulness* or *energetic resonance.* Because knowing via intuition, somatic sensation, emotion, and energetic resonance are private and personal ways to experience something, they are considered subjective. But, they are no less important tools for knowing a topic in rich detail.

Among the more challenging aspects of spending years in dissertation research and writing are two particularly de-motivating conditions: working in isolation, and feeling like no one in one's usual support system fully understands what we are going through. My (Deah's) solution to these conditions was to enlist Steve, a close friend, as a co-researcher to work with me during the last two years of dissertation process.

Steve worked as an interrater, performing all thematic content analysis in parallel to my own analysis. In addition, he proof-read every page of the pilot study report, candidacy essays, dissertation proposal, and dissertation.

Even more valuable, he offered excellent editorial suggestions that sharpened my writing, and deepened my thinking. He conducted some literature searches and turned up references I might not have found on my own. He discerned some flaws in the Organic Inquiry methodology, and suggested corrections that in our opinion enriches this emerging approach to human sciences research. He was not just a true co-researcher; throughout the years, he was a sounding board, a cheerleader, and nearly my alter ego.

Working so closely with a friend—himself not a doctoral student—could have been fraught with difficulties. Knowing each other well, we might have made assumptions that could have created confusion and hard feelings. I could have turned into an intolerable ogre—given the importance of the work to me—and he might have failed to meet the expectations I had that he could do the academic work. Our friendship could have been irreparably damaged by the stresses and uncertainties of a dissertation process. None of this happened.

In considering why the co-researcher process worked so well for us, we offer the following as a model for others.

1. We kept clear boundaries, communicating them continually. We were clear about role relationships; as the principal researcher, all design and process decisions were mine, but I encouraged input and critique, which

helped create his sense of ownership in the multiple projects.

2. I gave thorough directions, usually via email or attachments, leaving as much room as possible for Steve's independent creativity. When his analysis differed from mine, we looked at how we were separately looking at the data to see whether the difference was in the data itself, or in the lenses we were individually applying. This resolved worrisome discrepancies.

3. We were sensitive to each other's natural rhythms, work styles, and stress coping strategies. During one period I wrote during the day, he proofed and edited through the night, so I had little time lag in waiting for his feedback. When my desired timelines created too much pressure, we redistributed the workflow between us, or renegotiated the deadlines.

4. We made our friendship the priority. We gave each other space when needed, and helped each other with our lives outside of the research. We celebrated the ending of phases and projects.

Working with a co-researcher like I did may not be for everyone, and a co-researcher like I had may not be available, but it is a model for easily adding an additional evaluator for validity, as well as for dealing with isolation and the need for a strong support system that I can highly recommend.

Issues I'd Like to See Addressed in a Newsletter or on a Website about Organic Inquiry

To forward questions for possible inclusion in future materials on
Organic Inquiry, email: Publishers@LiminalRealities.com

103

Questions I'd Like to Ask about
Using Organic Inquiry for My Own Project

We'd love to hear from you about your research plans, and
we'd be interested in consulting with you about using Organic Inquiry.
See our website at www.LiminalRealities.com
for consultation policies and fees.
Students and faculty are encouraged to contact us at:
Publishers@LiminalRealities.com

CHAPTER 9

🍃

Specifics of One Complex
Organic Inquiry

This chapter gives a quick look at the methods guideline for one of our Organic Inquiry research designs. It is provided so that novice researchers can begin to imagine how they might structure their own project, and how various branches of the Organic approach—and the researcher's preferences of methods and procedures—can be intertwined. It is not our desire that other researchers simply replicate our design. However, it might be useful to see at least one example of how it has been done.

To more fully understand the purpose of some of the steps in the guideline, it may be helpful to have a bit of background about the study to which these procedures were applied. The formal research question was: *In an environment where clients are seeking healing, how does having a somatosensory experience identified as healing presence impact the experience of healing, what is changed in how clients view their world, and how might this, finally, impact healing?*

To begin to answer this question, we recruited eight interviewees who had experienced healing presence in connection with being a client of a naturopathic physician. The study was intentionally delimited to this population because of Deah's desire to address a knowledge gap in the clinical theory of naturopathic medicine. (A pilot study considered healing presence in non-human interactions.) Interviewees told their stories in hour long sessions, followed by producing a creative expression of their experience–a drawing, painting, or clay sculpture. We included a half day session with a resonance panel of three naturopathic physicians who provided some triangulation of data analysis. Interviewees then responded to some of the work produced by the resonance panel in order to achieved several layers of interactive reflexivity on the data analysis. Throughout the research period, we also performed our own data analysis, separately, and then compared and combined our findings into the final results.

Each step of the guideline below is annotated to indicate which principles of the Organic model it addresses. Commentary describes the details of how the step was applied in our study.

A Methods Guideline for One Organic Inquiry

1. *Create energetic container for the sacred, via appropriate shifts in consciousness prompted by setting a conducive internal and external atmosphere (sacred, chthonic, numinous)*

Each day of our research period, we set an energetic container for the sacred by way of performing our usual daily rituals, such as lighting candles. Prior to starting the work of the day—whether that was writing, interviewing, analysis, or other research tasks—the room was purified by chiming, smudging or movement and the Spirit guides and guardians of the research project were acknowledged and invited to be present. These guides and guardians were thanked and bade farewell at the end of each work day, or invited to stay to aid us in our work in the chthonic realm in our dreams on an ongoing basis. More than this was not necessary on most days, for each of our homes and work spaces already incorporated various meaningful Spiritual objects. On interview days, I (Deah) added more candles, and the lighting of tiny white holiday lights that had been strung around the entryway and down a hall leading into the interview room. Steve would simply "engage" with the various items of Spiritual significance in his space to focus his energies.

2. *Explicitly invite Spirit into procedures by holding a meditative intention, prayer chant, candle lighting, chiming, incense burning, or any of a number of Spiritual or symbolic practices (sacred, chthonic, numinous)*

When working with interviewees, Spirit was explicitly invited into the session by co-creating an altar at the beginning of the interview time. Each interviewee brought an item of Spiritual significance to add to the altar. Brief discussion of their items, and of what else was on the altar, set a nice tone of Spiritual sharing for the interview that followed. These Spiritual items returned home with the interviewees at the end of their sessions.

3. *In individual audio-taped sessions: (a) conduct simple discourse analysis during semi-structured interview by asking questions that promote reflective, critical, assumption-examining answers; (b) elicit embodied experience through meta-verbal data by using procedures of creative expression using clay or drawing; (c) debrief the process of creative expression (personal, relational, transformative).*

Our initial interview sessions were scheduled to run two hours. The first hour included co-creating an altar, and the interviewee telling her or his story, after which questions were asked from the semi-structured interview guide, or as prompted by the story itself. At the end of the first hour, interviewees were given a choice of music to accompany their creative expression activity, and a brief meditative moment was provided to assist in shifting from cognitive to tactile-intuitive modes. Most interviewees completed their creative expression within 30 minutes, allowing adequate time to explain their creative process and how it represented for them their experience of the topic under investigation. Items were retained by the researcher so that photographs could be taken. Clay items were baked by the researcher to increase their durability.

4. *Altar transcripts (transcribe tapes, indwell, rest, return, attain gestalt) and send to research associate to altar story through reading transcripts, indwelling, returning, attaining gestalt before*

beginning sequential analysis (sacred, chthonic, numinous, relational, transformative)

Where Moustakas (1990) used the term *indwelling* to indicate the process of attaining a deep, wholistic understanding of interviewees' stories, we use the term *altaring*, as in bringing to the altar of the sacred. Altaring normally lasted several days. In our studies, both of us separately entered a process of altaring, during which time we did not discuss the details of the interview or our impressions about the interviewees' story. Refraining from cross-talk allowed us to come into data analysis without each other's influence on our perceptions of what the data itself presented.

5. *Write vignettes and send to participants for review and approval. Ask interviewees to identify 3-5 key words from the vignette. Keep the interviewee-identified descriptors in separate data set. (sacred, chthonic, numinous, relational)*

Writing the vignettes was part of the altaring process for me (Deah) and a procedure that Steve did not participate in, as there was no need to write two different vignettes for each interviewee. It was also a type of analysis, in that in order to condense 20-35 pages of single spaced transcript it was necessary to make some decisions about what was at the heart of each story, what represented essential description about the topic of investigation, and what was tangential information.

Interviewees had the option to revise their vignette for accuracy and clarity if they chose to do so. Most did not. It was helpful to assure them that it was my intention to retain the flavor of their personalities as reflected in the idiosyncrasies of the spoken word, as this allowed some interviewees to resist rewriting their vignettes. Whereas in writing we have been taught to edit out redundant words, in speech these re-emphasized words become crucial data that needed to be preserved.

6. *Apply Chesler's sequential analysis (see Miles & Huberman (1994, p. 87) to transcripts for descriptors, themes, and categories, using Spirit and internal resonance as guides. Compare with research associate's results. Apply sequential*

*analysis to interviewee-identified descriptor-data set. Compare
to results from analyses on transcripts. (relational,
transformative)*

This was a complex and adapted use of Chesler's
procedures. We found that in doing each step, that sub-parts were
needed to keep us from losing track of where we were in the over-all
process. It helped to divide the analysis work into four phases: (1)
post-initial interview; (2) during resonance panel [see step 9 of this
guideline]; (3) post-resonance panel; and (4) post follow-up. The
diagram below depicts the parts of Phase One.

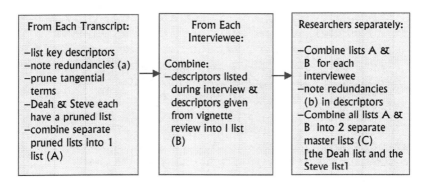

Figure 2. Phase One Sequential Content Analysis

Each step of identifying, noting, pruning, and combining
tended to take a whole day, and sometimes more, to ensure that all
essential descriptors were included. In general, we were able to
schedule interviews so that parts 1 and 2 of the Phase One analysis
were completed on the transcripts of each interview before the next
interview took place.

7. *In preparation for a resonance panel, generate 4 composite
    vignettes based on original interviewee vignettes, highlighting
    descriptors and themes from analysis to date. (relational,
    transformative)*

In order to disguise the identities of all interviewees, details
of individual stories were distributed over two or three composites.

This was done to preserve the anonymity of the interviewees. Each composite took about one day to write. Allowing this much time was necessary in order to ensure that an ample amount of descriptors were present in each composite, and that each vignette told a story that was in keeping with the stories we had heard from the interviewees.

Writing these composites was not only a cognitive-analytical exercise, but also each was a journey into the liminal domain, where the stories took on their own personalities, as if being told by four new interviewees.

8. *Conduct resonance panel with different participants to review exemplar vignettes, compare descriptors, develop synthesis statement, enrich dimensions of experience under investigation, and provide validity checks. Have panel note transformative shifts in vignettes, and in themselves from reading vignettes. (relational, chthonic, transformative)*

In this study we used a three person resonance panel to partially analyze interviewee data. The products of this analysis became data itself that was compared with the descriptors and themes developed from the combined interviewee data set noted in Phase One as list C. The work of the resonance panel constituted Phase Two of the content analysis. Its individual sub-parts are listed below.

```
            Resonance Panel

    -co-create altar
    -read composite vignettes
    -list key descriptors (D)
     found in composite vignettes
    -prune Phase One lists (C) of
     key interviewee descriptors
     to form list (E)
    -develop individual synthesis
     statements (1)
    -compare statements
    -develop group statement (2)
```

Figure 3. Phase Two Sequential Content Analysis

9. *Review with research associate feedback from the resonance panel, critically and reflectively compare to earlier descriptor lists, generate researchers' synthesis statements using Spirit and combined resonance as guide (relational, numinous, transformative)*

Up to this point Steve and I had worked separately, forming our own lists and categories, and identifying our own themes and category labels. With this step we entered Phase Three of the analysis process. In this phase we compared our separate analyses by looking at the categories we had each arrived at, finding the similarities and differences in themes, and using our own somatosensory resonances and dissonances—as well as much discussion—to guide us in merging our individual results into collaborative findings. The details of this work are illustrated in Figure 4 below.

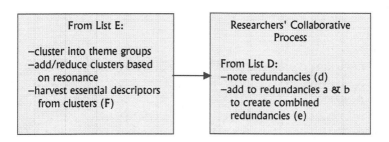

Figure 4. Phase Three Sequential Content Analysis

10. *In second brief interview with interviewees, review and ask for response to synthesis statement / findings to date. Responses form the report of transformative changes of heart. Draw questions from first interviews: this is what happened for you; this is what you said about it; how have you changed since this experience; what if anything has shifted for you from participating in this research. (personal, relational, transformative)*

Follow-up interviews lasted about one hour. Creative expression items, which had been professionally photographed in the interim, were returned at this time. Details of the interview were reviewed and clarification questions asked. This interview focused on the transformative changes that had occurred in the lives of interviewees as associated with their experiencing of the topic under investigation. A second area of interest focused on transformative changes that had occurred in connection with participating in the research project. Interviewees used their several subjectivities as tools of knowing during this session to select which synthesis statement written by the resonance panel best captured the essence of their experience. The follow-up session was the first part of Phase Four of the data analysis process.

Interviewees
−review panel's synthesis statements (1) & (2) −using resonance, select most descriptive of own experience −offer brief analysis about other statements −reflect on transformative changes

Figure 5. Step One of Phase Four Sequential Content Analysis

11. *Generate synthesis statements with research associate, using combined resonance, journeys into the liminal realm, and consistency with personal experience as guides (personal, relational, transformative, chthonic, numinous)*

Based on our own individual understandings of the findings we had generated in this project, each of us wrote our own synthesis statements. Keeping in mind the several synthesis statements that had been written by the resonance panel, we then compared those statements, and crafted one joint statement to represent our mutual understanding of what the sum total of the data had told us.

As part of this step, which was Part Two of Phase Four (see Figure 5 on page 81), we also discussed the interviewees' responses to the resonance panel's synthesis statements, and took into consideration their reflections on how the panel's statements did or did not capture the essence of their own experiences.

Although one more step was included on the method guideline, the data analysis work was completed at this point.

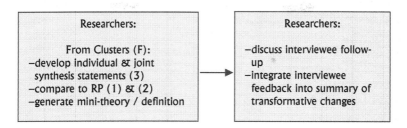

| Researchers:

From Clusters (F):
–develop individual & joint
  synthesis statements (3)
–compare to RP (1) & (2)
–generate mini-theory / definition | Researchers:

–discuss interviewee follow-
  up
–integrate interviewee
  feedback into summary of
  transformative changes |

Figure 6. Step Two of Phase Four Sequential Content Analysis

12. *Review personal and interpersonal experience of participating in research with research associate. Discuss any transformative learnings and changes of heart that have occurred for us individually, and in our collaborative relationship. Generate report of transformative change. (personal, relational, transformative)*

This item is listed in the method guideline to indicate just one of the many (and frequent) reflexive conversations we had about our own experiences during the research period. This step—with the exception of generating the final report—actually occurred throughout the project as one way we kept the workload manageable and kept ourselves and our relationship healthy. More about how we worked together is given in Chapter 8.

As we have stated, this guideline was generated to help us stay on track with our own complex research project.   Other researchers should develop a guideline that fits their own study and purposes. It is our hope that in presenting our guideline here it can serve as just one example, or as a point of departure, for how many different elements and ways of knowing can be incorporated into an Organic Inquiry.

Pieces to incorporate into my research design:

What the steps of my research plan might look like:

CHAPTER 10

🍃

Some Final Thoughts

As the reader might surmise from the material in this book, using the Organic Inquiry methodology is no easy way to perform qualitative research. While it has certain appeal for researchers who wish to incorporate the sacred and a partnership with Spirit into a disciplined way of knowing, the demands on researchers are as rigorous as any other methodology for human sciences research. Still, the novice researcher need not be overly intimidated by the opportunity to help establish the Organic approach as a viable option in the range of innovative methodologies.

Having used this approach in three separate projects ourselves, and having paid close attention to the difficulties and frustrations we encountered, we offer the following suggestions to other novice researchers for navigating the chthonic and liminal realms of the Organic Inquiry.

If something does not seem to be working, use an "act as if" approach, and it will generally fall in place. Even if you are not sure you are in contact with Spirit, in our view you always are. So when you act like it is true in time it will be. It is both a psychological and Spiritual technique, and it works.

In other words, when something seems to be awry, this might be viewed as one of the tests and challenges presented by the chthonic realm, or the research trickster (Anderson, 1998, 2000). You might consider this as a time when your trust in yourself, in your ability as a researcher, is in some way being investigated by your partner: Spirit. A solution might be to recognize the perception of being off-course as an opportunity to critically evaluate what you have planned, how you are operationalizing your plan, and where adjustments need to be made.

Trust your self. Get out of your way, shut off. Stop thinking, stop your mind and let all your senses work. Use your intuition by simply allowing it to inform you. This is not an active approach but a receptive one, and to be successful you must give in to it.

We cannot emphasize enough the importance of trusting yourself, and using all your subjectivities as tools of knowing. Organic Inquiry gives us permission to do both. In fact it encourages us to use both.

Be careful not to start analyzing data until it tells you to. That is, give adequate time to altaring the stories of your participants. Your conscious mind will continually try to jump in and hijack the project. Keeping it occupied with the things it actually does have to do will help nurture it and allow it to feel like it has a place in your work and being so it will not need to attempt to intrude so much.

Even though in our projects we began data analysis while still collecting data from more interviewees (and we refer the reader back to Chapter 8 to see how carefully we did that), the indwelling—or, *altaring,* as we called it—step is vitally important to the Organic approach. It might be said that it is the mind that wants to rush into analysis, but the heart and Spirit have the need to rest in the storied nature of the data collected before it is deconstructed, manipulated, categorized, and nomothetically rendered. So, even though your mind may demand attention, you can tell it to quiet down and give it some of its own work to do as mentioned above. Your subconscious intuitive abilities will already be at work, and allowing them to move freely without interference from an overactive mind allows Spirit to move more freely. It is very important that you do not block the flow of energy.

Keep it simple. There will always be plenty to do.

As we have shown in Chapter 7, an Organic Inquiry generates an enormous volume of data. The more simple your research design and your procedures are, the easier the project will be to manage. Just interviewing and transcribing audio tapes verbatim is overwhelmingly time consuming and tiring. After that, data analysis may seem to go on forever. Breaking the project into phases, as we did, helps to stay focused and to be revitalized from each new step, and by frequent trips into the liminal domain to gather not only data, but also confidence, serenity, and renewal.

Breath is the most effective tool to use to shift into an altered state, and will most likely become more effective the more it is attempted. If you are having trouble quieting the mind and letting go with simple breathing techniques you can try using music and movement.

Music is perhaps the single most significant way to immediately experience Spirit in the body, as opposed to the mind. Since in our view the Organic approach values embodying the methodology, doing something that moves your awareness into the body will help embody the work, energize you and relax your mind to move you into an heightened consciousness.

If this is the case, using instrumental music can be helpful, as can music that invites you to chant or use a wordless humming or vocalizing that will resonate through your body's energy centers. Some of our favorites include Native American flutes and drumming, Asian meditation or healing music or gentle piano music.

For some, a more active approach may be called for and drumming for yourself, playing music that is more intense or free form dance and energy movements (such as qi gong or tai ji) may be helpful. The point is to move out of your normal ordinary state of mind into an extraordinary state.

The underworld of the chthonic realm may seem scary, but remember: It is a part of who you are, and it is safe for you to explore it.

Although it is likely that persons who are attracted to the Organic methodology will have some experience with exploring their subconscious mind and their shadow issues, it is possible that the concept of the underworld of the chthonic domain engenders a different level of willingness because popular and cultural mythologies make out the underworld to be such a dark, mysterious, dangerous, unsavory part of the psyche.

In our view, it is not only instructive, but healthful, to explore this part of ourselves in the context of an Organic Inquiry. This gives you the opportunity of valuing all parts of yourself and letting even those "dark" parts aid you in your work. Doing so brings more of oneself into the research, and ensures that the findings are thoroughly grounded in the wholism of the researchers' (and participants') experience.

If this still frightens you, try asking for a guide or ally to travel with you into the underworld, to aid you in your quest and protect you from any fears you might discover, or that you carry with you. When you ask, do not be afraid to embrace whatever image first appears to you. This is usually the one who will help you. Trust in yourself, but ask for help if you need it.

Take time to always enjoy yourself.

Remember, enjoying the work is one way of being in partnership with Spirit. If the work of research is not enjoyable, we would say that the researchers' heart and Spirit are being left out of the process. And if this is the case, the principles of the Organic methodology are not being as fully applied as they could be.

Taking breaks and consciously stepping away from the work and doing something fun and relaxing – something that really takes your attention off your work – will pay off with your revitalized return to your project. It is part of the methodology to do this, so there is no need for the guilt that can so easily plague us when we are so intensely involved in research, perhaps with deadlines hovering over us that we fear we will not be able to meet. This may be hard for some dedicated scholars, so we mention it to remind you of the interconnectedness of your life to the work. It is all one.

If you are working with others, or even alone, make your health the priority, not the research. If you keep yourself healthy the work will flow naturally of its own accord and you will be okay.

Tackling any significant research project can be very stressful. When the study is a dissertation project, or a work-related or grant-funded project, the stakes for success can be overwhelming. We found that much of this stress was dissipated because we made the project secondary to sustaining our own physical, emotional, Spiritual, and relationship health. Then because we interacted with our projects from this position of priority on health, we were able to easily deal with the various stresses that the projects created. We found that encouraging one another to take a break here and there was helpful. This is also another advantage to having a research associate to help remind you that there are other aspects of your life that need your attention besides the research.

You should feel free to talk about things with your co-researchers, though you should be mindful to choose just what you talk about to whom. If there are problems or stuck places, talking will often release them.

Principal researchers can benefit from having co-researchers with whom to share the burdens of thinking through problems and dilemmas. Each person will have their unique perspectives on the work and taking advantage of this and including them both makes them feel more included and also makes the methodology more effective.

Keep the energy moving. If you are stuck somewhere, move on to something else and come back later with rested, fresh eyes Trying to push through stuck energy will often backfire on you and end up in frustration.

It is important to keep the energy moving in your whole life. Do not try to make it all happen within the confines of the project itself or you will be placing undue burdens on the work and may negatively impact the process. Would you try to pull a tree out of the ground to make it grow faster? Of course not. The same is true of the Organic approach. It takes its own time to grow.

No matter what data analysis method one incorporates into an Organic Inquiry, there will be periods when it seems not to flow smoothly. Having some alternate things to do during these times can keep one's mind from getting numb. Some of these alternate things might be research related, others might encourage you to take a well-timed and well-deserved break. Plowing through until you are done might not be the best solution.

Be prepared to encounter skepticism about using an emerging research methodology. Don't worry; it is good for you. The more you are challenged, the more you will become confident about why Organic Inquiry is a great approach to human sciences research.

Skeptics and supporters alike are correct to challenge us about the validity and generalizability of the findings generated from Organic inquiries, just as they should if we were using any other methodology. Though it may on occasion be frustrating to seem to have to defend your work, in the end it will strengthen both you and the methodology to do so. It is when you can stay centered in the process despite distraction that you will know you are on the correct path.

References

NOTE: First names are given when known to help the reader locate these resources more readily.

Acker, J., Barry, K., & Esseveld, J. (1991). Objectivity and truth: Problems in doing feminist research. In M. M. Fonow & J. A. Cook (Eds.), *Beyond methodology: Feminist scholarship as lived research* (pp. 133-153). Bloomington, IN: Indiana University Press.

Anderson, Rosemary (1998). Intuitive inquiry: A transpersonal approach. In Braud, W., & Anderson, R. (Eds.). *Transpersonal research methods for the social sciences: Honoring human experience*, 66-94. Thousand Oaks, CA: Sage Publications.

Anderson, Rosemary (2000). Intuitive Inquiry: Interpreting objective and subjective data. In *Revision: Journal of Consciousness and Transformation, 22,* (4), 31-39.

Braud, W. (1998). An expanded view of validity. In W. Braud & R. Anderson (Eds.), *Transpersonal research methods for the social sciences: Honoring human experience*, pp. 213-237. Thousand Oaks, CA: Sage Publications.

Behar, R. (1996). *The Vulnerable Observer: Anthropology That Breaks Your Heart.* Boston: Beacon Press.

Benor, D. J. (1984). Fields and energies related to healing: A review of Soviet and western studies. *Psi Research, 3* (1), 21-35.

Benor, D. J. (2001). *Spiritual healing as the energy side of Einstein's equation.* Retrieved May 24, 2003 from http://www.wholistichealing research.com/Articles/Einstein.htm.

Benson, H. (2000). *The relaxation response.* [Reissue ed.]. New York: Harper Collins/Avon.

Bohm, David 1980. *Wholeness and the Implicate Order.* Boston: Routledge & K. Paul.

Briggs, J. P., & Peat, F. D. (1984). *Looking glass universe: The emerging science of wholeness.* New York: Simon & Schuster/Touchstone.

Clements, Jennifer (2000). *Organic Inquiry: Theory.* Unpublished manuscript.

Clements, Jennifer (2001). *Organic Inquiry: Researching in Partnership with Spirit.* Unpublished manuscript.

Clements, Jennifer; Ettling, Dorothy; Jenett, Dianne; & Shields, Lisa (1998). *Organic Inquiry: If Research Were Sacred.* Palo Alto, CA: Serpentine Press.

Creswell, J. W. (1994). *Research methods and design: Qualitative & quantitative approaches.* Thousand Oaks: Sage Publications.

Curry, D. (2003). *Healing Presence: Experiencing the medicine of the naturopathic client-clinician relationship.* Doctoral dissertation, Saybrook Graduate School and Research Center, San Francisco. Dissertations Express, 3094683.

Dallimore, E. J. (2000). A feminist response to issues of validity in research. *Women's Studies in Communication, 23* (2), 157-181. Retrieved 30 April, 2003, from Proquest Psychology Journals database.

DeQuincey, C. (2000). *Radical nature: consciousness all the way down— integrating different worldviews on mind and body through a radical revision of ontology and epistemology, recognizing the primacy of process, feeling, and intersubjectivity.* Unpublished doctoral dissertation, California Institute of Integral Studies, San Francisco.

Elias, D. (1997). It's time to change our minds: an introduction to transformative learning. *ReVision: A Journal of Consciousness and Transformation, 20* (1), 2-5.

Ferrer, J. N. (2002). *Revisioning transpersonal theory: A participatory vision of human Spirituality.* Albany, NY: State University of New York Press.

Gee, J.P. (1986). Unitsin the production of narrative discourse. Discourse Processes, 9, 391-422. In Riessman, C.K. (1993), *Narrative Analysis,* Qualitative Research Methods Series 30, Thousand Oaks, CA: A Sage University Paper.

Gendlin, E. T. (1978). *Focusing.* New York: Bantam New Age Book.

Gendlin, Eugene T (1997). *Experiencing and the Creation of Meaning: A Philosophical and Psychological Approach to the Subjective (Rev Ed.).* Evanston, IL: Northwestern University Press.

Giorgi, A. (1989). Learning and memory from the perspective of phenomenological psychology. In R. Valle & S. Halling (Eds.), *Existential-phenomenological perspectives in psychology* (pp. 99-112). New York: Plenum Press.

Hall, W. A., & Calley, P. (2001). Enhancing the rigor of grounded theory: Incorporating reflexivity and relationality. *Qualitative Health Research, 11* (2), 257-272. Retrieved April 30, 2003, from Proquest Psychology Journals database

Heger, H. (1980). *The men with the pink triangles.* (D. Fernbach, Trans.) Boston: Alyson Publications. [Original work published 1980, Hamburg, Germany: Merlin-Verlag]

Heron, John (1996). *Co-Operative Inquiry: Research into the Human Condition.* London: Sage Publications.

Hills, C. (Ed.). (1977). *Energy, matter and form: Towards a science of consciousness.* Boulder Creek, CA: University of the Trees Press.

Holstein, J.A. & Gubrium, J.F. *(1995). The Active Interview.* Qualitative Research Method Series 37, Thousand Oaks, CA: Sage Publications.

Kaptchuk, T. J. (2000). *The web that has no weaver: Understanding Chinese medicine (2nd ed.).* Lincolnwood, IL: Contemporary Books.

Kremer, J. (1999). Healing and cosmology: Recovering ancestral healing ways for the future. In press. K. Kailo, (Ed.), *Indigenous Healing Approaches.*

Kvale, S. (1996). *InterViews: An Introduction to Qualitative Research Interviewing.* Thousand Oaks, CA: Sage Publications.

Labov, W. (Ed.) (1972). The transformation of experience in narrative syntax. In Riessman, C.K. (1993), *Narrative Analysis,* Qualitative Research Methods Series 30, Thousand Oaks, CA: A Sage University Paper.

Lounsberry, Joyce. (2001). *The power of the drum: A multicultural journey into Spiritual transformations and mind-body healing experienced by eight professional women drummers.* Doctoral dissertation, The Institute of Transpersonal Psychology.

Lyons, A. (1999). Shaping health psychology: Qualitative research, evaluation and presentation. In M.Murray & K. Chamberlain (Eds.)., *Qualitative health psychology: Theories and methods.* (pp. 241-255). London: Sage Publications.

Malterud, K. (1993). Shared understanding of the qualitative research process: Guidelines for the medical researcher. *Family Practice, 10,* 201-06.

Malterud, K. (2001). Qualitative research: Standards, challenges, and guidelines. *The Lancet, 359* (9280), 483-488. Retrieved April 30, 2003, from Proquest Psychology Journals database.

Maslow, A. H. (1970, September/October). Peak experiences in education and art. *The Humanist,* 29-31.

Maughan and Reason (2001). A Cooperative Inquiry into Deep Ecology. *ReVision: A Journal of Consciousness and Transformation, 23,* (4), 18-24.

Mezirow, J. (1997, Fall). Transformation theory out of context. [Electronic version]. *Adult Education Quarterly, 48* (1). Retrieved October, 2001, from http://www.proquest.com

Mezirow, J. (1998, Spring). On critical reflection. [Electronic version]. *Adult Education Quarterly, 48* (3). Retrieved October, 2001, from http://www.proquest.com

Miles, M. B., & Huberman, A. M. (1994). *Qualitative data analysis: An expanded sourcebook,* (2nd ed.). Thousand Oaks, CA: Sage Publications.

Mitchell, Carolyn Finn. (2000). *Women and nature: Connection to animals and Spirit experienced by Celtic-Irish women.* Doctoral dissertation, Institute of Transpersonal Psychology. Dissertation Abstracts International, 61(04), 2274B.

Moustakas, Clark (1990). *Heuristic Research: Design, Methodology, and Application.* Thousand Oaks, CA: Sage Publications.

Moss, Richard (1986). *The black butterfly: an invitation to radical aliveness.* Berkeley, CA: Celestial Arts.

Naess, Arne (1973). *The Shallow and the Deep, Long-Range Ecological Movements: A Summary.* Inquiry, 16 (1), 95-100.

Nagata, A. L. (2000). Resonant connections. *ReVision: A Journal of Consciousness and Transformation, 22* (4), 24-31.

Neilsen, JM (1990). *Feminist Research Methods.* Boulder, CO: Westview Press.

Neuberger, M. (1932). The doctrine of the healing power of nature throughout the course of time. *Journal of the American Institute of Homeopathy, 25* (8), 861-884. L.J. Boyd, (Trans).

Newton, Susan. (1996). *Exploring the interstices: The space between in the body/mind disciplines of Aikido and fencing.* Unpublished doctoral dissertation, Institute of Transpersonal Psychology, Palo Alto, CA.

Packer, M. J., & Addison, R. B. (1989). *Entering the circle: Hermeneutic investigation in psychology.* Albany, NY: State University of New York Press.

Phelon, C. (2001). *Healing presence: An intuitive inquiry into the presence of the psychotherapist.* Unpublished doctoral dissertation. Institute of Transpersonal Psychology, Palo Alto, CA.

Pierrakos, J. C. (1990). *Core energetics.* Mendocino, CA: LifeRhythm Publication.

Pinard, Rose Anne. (2000). *Integrative dialogue: From fragmentation to a reverential unfolding of wholeness and mutuality.* Doctoral dissertation, The California School of Professional Psychology. Dissertation Abstracts International 61(08), 4478B.

Polkinghorne, D.E. (1988). *Narrative Knowing and the Human Sciences.* Albany, NY: SUNY Press.

Richards, Ruth (1996). *Does the Lone Genius Ride Again? Chaos, Creativity, and Community.* Journal of humanistic Psychology, 36 (2), 44-60.

Richards, Ruth (2000). *Millennium as Opportunity: Chaos, Creativity, and Guilford's Structure of Intellect Model.* Creativity Research Journal, 13 (3 & 4), 249-265.

Richards, Ruth (2001). *A New Aesthetic for Environmental Awareness: Chaos Theory, the Beauty of Nature, and Our Broader Humanistic Identity.* Journal of humanistic Psychology, 41 (2), 59-95.

Riessman, C.K. (1993). *Narrative analysis.* Qualitative Research Methods Series 30, A Sage University Paper. Thousand Oaks, CA: Sage.

Rode, Maja A. (2000). *What is beauty? A living inquiry for mind and heart.* Doctoral dissertation, Institute of Transpersonal Psychology, 2000). UMI, 9969181.

Rothberg, Donald (1994). *Spiritual Inquiry.* In ReVision: Journal of Consciousness and Transformation.

Rubin, H.J. & Rubin, I.S. (1995). *Qualitative Interviewing: The Art of Hearing Data.* Thousand Oaks, CA: Sage Publications.

Runco & Richards, Ruth. (1997). *Eminent Creativity, Everyday Creativity, and Health.* Greenwich, CT: Ablex.

Sheldrake, R. (1995). *A new science of life: The hypothesis of morphic resonance.* Rochester, VT: Park Street Press.

Shields, Lisa. (1996). *The experience of beauty, body image and the feminine in three generations of mothers and daughters.* Unpublished doctoral dissertation, Institute of Transpersonal Psychology, Palo Alto, CA.

Smith, T. (2000). *A hermeneutic-phenomenological exploration of person-to-person authentic encounters.* Unpublished proposal for doctoral dissertation, Saybrook Graduate School and Research Center, San Francisco.

Starhawk, (1997). *Dreaming the Dark: Magic, Sex, and Politics (15th anniversary edition).* Boston: Beacon Press.

Tarnas, R; Laszlo, E; Gablik, S; & Perez-Christi, A (2001). *The Cosmic World: How We Participate in Thee and Thou in Us.* ReVision: a Journal of Consciousness and Transformation, 23 (3), 42-48.

Tart, C. T. (1971). Scientific foundations for the study of altered states of consciousness. *Journal of Transpersonal Psychology, 3* (2), 93-124.

Tart, C. T. (1977). Science, states of consciousness, and Spiritual experiences. The need for state-specific sciences. In C. T. Tart (Ed.)., *Transpersonal psychologies* (pp. 9-58). New York: Harper & Row.

Tart, C. T. (1983). *States of consciousness.* El Cerrito, CA: Psychological Processes.

Tiller, W. A. (1975). *Energy fields and the human body, part 2.* Retrieved May 24, 2003 from http://www.tiller.org/energyfields.

Tiller, W. A. (1999). Science and medicine. [Electronic version]. *Subtle Energies, 6* (3). Retrieved May 25, 2003, from http://www. tiller.org/subtle-energies.html

Tiller, W. A. (2001). *Subtle energy actions and physical domain correlations.* Retrieved May 25, 2003, from http://www.biomindsuperpowers.com/Pages/SubtleEnergyActions.html

Ussher, J. M. (1999). Feminist approaches to qualitative health research. In M. Murray & K. Chamberlain (Eds.), *Qualitative health psychology: Theories and methods* (pp. 98-114). Thousand Oaks, CA: Sage Publications.

Van Manen, M (1990). *Researching Lived Experience: Human Science for an Action Sensitive Pedagogy.* Albany, NY: State University of New York Press.

Walsh, Roger (1990). *The Spirit of Shamanism.* New York: Jeremy Tarcher/Putnam.

Washburn, M. (1995). *The ego and the dynamic ground.* (2nd ed.). Albany, NY: State University of New York Press.

Wilbur, K. (1990). *Eye to eye: The quest for a new paradigm.* Boston: Shambhala.

Wolf, F. A. (1999). *The Spiritual universe: One physicist's vision of Spirit, soul, matter, and self.* Portsmouth, NH: Moment Point Press.

Zukav, G. (1980). *The dancing Wu Li masters: An overview of the new physics.* New York: Bantam New Age Books.

GLOSSARY

Given here are definitions of the most frequently used terms in this book. In some cases we have borrowed definitions from others' work when their meaning is clear and in alignment with how we use the term. At other times we have developed working definitions for our own studies. To facilitate easy retrieval, the terms are given in alphabetical order, although this does not reflect their relative importance to the topics of the Organic Inquiry Primer.

Altaring --- akin to the notion of *indwelling* in Heuristic Inquiry, an immersion process of being with data prior to performing any analytic procedures; allowing the subjective impact of data itself and the experiences of seeking rapport and empathic attunement associated with gathering the data to seep through layers of consciousness while held as a sacred trust, before imposing reductive or objectifying analysis methods to the data.

Audit trail --- a log, diary, or other collection of records that document actions taken, obstacles encountered and how they were resolved, dilemmas pondered, etc as the research proceeds.

Cosmology --- the study of the philosophies and physics of understanding the natural universe, including the role of humans and their conceptualizations of and interactions with the Sacred.

Disciplined knowing --- the process of attaining knowledge in a systematic and systemic manner, using objective and subjective approaches and procedures.

Empathic attunement --- the condition of sharing, connecting, or being in the moment with another person; in the context of this book, being in the moment with research participants during interviews and other procedures, and connecting on a personal level with the information participants bring forward.

Environmental qi --- the subtle energies present in any given natural location, such as mountains, water, weather, plants, humans or animals as well as those emanating, from colors, shapes, artwork, buildings, streets and other artifacts of the built world, etc.

Epistemology --- the study of processes of knowing; how we know that we know.

Ethnobiographic --- an approach to research that is commonly found in the field of cultural anthropology; it focuses on the ethnic aspects of the lives of individuals, families, and groups, and how ethnicity informs and shapes personal psychology and interpersonal responses in the larger society.

Exemplar vignettes --- composite, abbreviated stories composed of verbatim phrasings, constructed to serve as representative but unidentifiable examples of participant interviews, read by a second level group of participants.

Experiential knowing --- the process of attaining understanding through personal experience; a *learn by doing* method.

Experients --- persons who experience a situation or phenomenon under investigation.

Femininist --- in the context of this book, feminist implies an orientation that aims to emancipate understandings and experients from stereotypes and from ignorance due to as yet undiscovered knowledge. It equally privileges feminine and masculine approaches to understanding, as well as seeking to integrate multicultural perspectives.

Generative knowledge --- understandings that lead to further facts, and testable theories.

Hermaneutic -- that which searches for the meaning and meaningfulness of an experience. As a research method, it is most commonly used in studies of sacred texts and qualitiative psychological research.

Heuristic --- that which is self-designing, self-evaluating, and self-correcting. As a research method, it is commonly used in psychological explorations of one's own psyche or experience.

Indigenous --- in the context of this book, pertaining to tribal (aboriginal) paradigms that promote sustainable ecology in all aspects of living. All things are considered to be alive, sacred, equal and interconnected. (see Participatory Paradigm).

Idiographic knowing --- information about a subject that is multi-layered, rich in description, may contain both objective and subjective observation and description, and is drawn from the unique experiences of individuals, as opposed to being developed from statistical averages in which individuality is erased.

Liminal domain --- the between place; threshold area; the subconsciousness in which phenomena are perceived but unarticulated.

Method --- a set of specific procedures for pursuing diciplined knowing.

Methodology --- an overarching philosophy that guides the research approach taken.

Modernist view --- the set of principles, assumptions, actions, etc, that proceed from the belief that there is an inviolate separateness of various realms, that only that which is perceivable by the five senses, rational, and empirically provable is real.

Normative view --- the common use of unexamined understanding; the received, presumed standard.

Ontology --- the study of reality; how we decide what is real.

Organic --- natural; having a life and growth cycle that is innate to itself. In research, making use of natural and holistic ways of knowing.

Participatory paradigm --- the set of principles, actions, assumptions, etc, that proceed from the belief that everything is connected and has a degree of consciousness, and that humans have responsibilities to maintain the natural order of life. (see *Indigenous*)

Postmodern --- the term used to indicate the contemporary era that began in the last quarter of the 20th century as the assumptions, values, and philosophies of the industrial-capitalist age started to be replaced by the growing and overlapping paradigms of connectivity, sustainability, and social responsibility.

PsychoSpiritual --- that which is a combination of emotion and Spirit, or of psychological approaches to things of a Spiritual nature.

Qi --- in traditional Chinese medicine, the subtle energy of the life force, taking any one of several specific actions in the body and in the natural world; formerly transliterated as *chi*.

Qigong – formerly transliterated as chi kung, a broad system of methods and practices for self healing that emphasize energy flows; part of Daoist (Taoist) Spirituality, a system that is primarily about energy and balance.

Sacred --- that which promotes, contains or embodies the life-affirming, healing, transformative dynamics of one's relationship to the circle of life, that has the quality of reverential respect toward the indwelling of Spirit. A qualitative state of the presence of Spirit.

Somatosensory --- the physical sensations felt in the body; used to classify a type of experience and a way of knowing that occurs through bodily felt awareness.

Spirit --- the living energy of the great mysterious, an ever-active catalyst that is life unfolding. An embodying creative force.

Spiritual --- a state of consciousness wherein one recognizes a reality that is greater than the mundane material realm. Any attitude or practice whereby one feels, thinks, or acts with reverence for that which is sacred.

Subtle energy or energies --- forces that "have no amplitude or frequency but were known for their effects, [and] have yet to be directly measured, or consensually observed" (Feinstein, 2001, p. 2).

Taiji --- formerly transliterated as *t'ai chi*, a set of specific movements designed to promote mental, physical and Spiritual balance and well being; developed originally as *t'ai chi chuan*, a martial art for self defense, taiji has evolved into a form of healing meditation.

Transformative --- a quality of difference that occurs in a shift from one set of assumptions or way of being to another, whereby an essential condition or character of a person is changed in a lasting and profound way.

Transparent --- transparency in research is the making of all procedures explicit and reproducible so that biases and errors can be observed by others.

Transpersonal --- a branch of psychology that looks beyond (trans) the individual to the role of the Spiritual, sacred, mythic, archetypal, and symbolic in human behavior, desire, and wellbeing.

Triangulating --- the process of comparing data acquired from one set of procedures with data obtained from a different method in order to achieve multiple confirmations of reliability of data.

Vignette --- an abbreviated version of an interview; the heart of a participant's story; usually verbatim in what is included, with redundancies and perceived irrelevancies omitted.

What Students are Saying about Organic Inquiry

I was drawn to Organic Inquiry primarily because this methodology places a premium on feelings as a legitimate source of data as cognition. I wanted to employ a narrative method that enabled researcher reflexivity at a holistic level drawing from and making explicit subconscious processes that have shaped and influenced the research journey. Investigating the human-companion animal bond in relation to terminal prognosis euthanasia was enmeshed with sensitivities and ethical questioning. The primer acted as a guide, in itself it generated an Organic process as I struggled to find my voice as an emergent researcher. Using the primer in this way enabled me to embrace the methodology fully. Mapping my own personal transformation throughout the process of my Doctoral study was made possible through keeping a reflexive process journal, dream journaling, stream of consciousness writing and through expressive art. I lived the methodology and as result new realities were opened up for me. I had intended to enter academia full-time on completion of my Doctorate study but the journey through the study has left me in a very different place, new priorities have emerged for living my life personally and professionally. The primer enabled the process that was the catalyst for this. It has been essential in my working and invaluable in my own metamorphosis as a researcher.

Susan Elisabeth Dawson
School of Health and Social Change
Manchester Metropolitan University
United Kingdom

I have chosen Organic Inquiry because it begins with an assumption that all things are sacred and interconnected. This assumption corresponds to the concept of 'oneness' and the relationship between people and the Universe as put forward in the quantum physics research. Since my investigation is about me consciously partnering with Spirit or the Universe, it is imperative that my research methodology be able to accommodate this. Transformational learning is an explicit goal of Organic Inquiry; such a methodology fits my research question which is to make explicit the story of my lived experience of transformation.

Duanita Eleniak
Consciousness Studies
International University of Professional Studies
Hawaii

About the Authors

Deah Curry PhD, holds a doctorate in psychology from Saybrook Graduate School and Research Center in San Francisco. She was the first student at Saybrook to use the Organic Inquiry methodology, and her work earned the Dissertation with Distinction for 2003. She is currently an adjunct instructor at Bastyr University near Seattle teaching psychoSpiritually oriented courses to naturopathic medicine and midwifery students. With Steve, Deah revised her dissertation as a trade book for the psychology and naturopathic medicine audience under the title *Healing Presence: Bodily Felt Experiencings of Transpersonal Connection in*  *Naturopathic and Non-Clinical Settings,* published by Infinity. When she isn't teaching or writing, Deah works with women who are struggling with the emotions of health crises or chronic illness, helping them to reconnect with their life force. The mission of her counseling practice—*InnerJourneyWork*—is to be a creative catalyst for deep self-awareness, courageous self-development, and revitalized self-healing.

 ***Steven J Wells*** is a self directed, life long learner, with an academic background in multidisciplinary studies and wholistic environmental design, and long standing interests in such topics as cultural anthropology, philosophy, transpersonal and humanistic psychology, Spirituality, non-ordinary states of consciousness, and healing. His professional experience includes producing events for a cutting-edge gay cultural arts collective, managing a rural food co-operative while homesteading on 40 acres, (without a mule), and creating and directing a non-profit healing arts community center in Seattle, WA, where a wide range of transformative experiences were encountered by diverse participants. As an informal independent scholar, Steve is currently engaged in a longitudinal, heuristic study of the interplay of mental and physical disorders and related psychoSpiritual states of consciousness. He loves spending time with plants and in nature.

Healing Presence
Bodily Felt Experiencings of
Transpersonal Connection in
Naturopathic and Non-Clinical Settings

This book presents the results of two related Organic Inquiries in a non-academic format. Fifteen stories of real people and their extraordinary experiences with a life changing phenomenon that helped them revitalize their sense of balance and healing are given. Interspersed with these stories are research findings that identify essential interactional characteristics that mindful clinicians will want to develop, or avoid, in their journey towards becoming a healing presence. The stories also serve to illustrate more didactic discussions of topics that contribute to understanding the psychoSpiritual nature of healing, such as suffering, empathy and compassion, subtle energy and resonance, bodily felt and direct knowing, the vitalist tradition in medicine, and Spiritual emergency.

And keep an eye on these websites for
future books from Deah Curry PhD and Steven J Wells:

www.BuyBooksOnTheWeb.com
www.Amazon.com
www.LiminalRealities.com

Liminal   Realities

Kirkland WA

Made in the USA
Lexington, KY
05 October 2016